Prince George

"Partners in Progress" by Maureen Keibel
Produced in co-operation with the
Prince George Chamber of Commerce
Windsor Publications Ltd.
Burlington, Ontario

Prince George
Rivers, Railways, and Timber
Bev Christensen

*To my mother, Winnie Russell, whose patient support
made it possible for me to write this book.*

Windsor Publications, Ltd.—History Books Division
Managing Editor: Karen Story
Design Director: Alexander D'Anca

Staff for *Prince George: Rivers, Railways, and Timber*
Manuscript Editor: Doreen Nakakihara
Photo Editor: Loren Prostano
Editor, Corporate Profiles: Judith Hunter
Production Editor, Corporate Profiles: Albert Polito
Editorial Assistants: Kim Kievman, Michael Nugwynne, Kathy B. Peyser, Theresa J. Solis
Publisher's Representative, Corporate Profiles: Hughes Winfield
Design and Layout: Christina L. Rosepapa
Layout Artist, Corporate Profiles: Michael Burg
Production Assistant: Bonnie Felt

Windsor Publications, Ltd.
Elliot Martin, Chairman of the Board
James L. Fish III, Chief Operating Officer
Michele Sylvestro, Vice President / Sales-Marketing

*Previous page: The city
lights of Prince George twin-
kle beneath an evening sky.
Photo by Bob Clarke*

CONTENTS

A colorful sunset silhouettes the Cameron Street bridge. Photo by Bob Clarke

PREFACE

Since Prince George has been my home for most of my life, I approached the task of researching and writing this book with considerable enthusiasm.

I soon discovered, despite my first-hand knowledge of the subject, it was often necessary to call on others in the community for assistance. It is with gratitude that I say the support, interest, and encouragement I received from these people eased my task immeasurably.

I would particularly like to thank Kent Sedgwick, who assisted in the research of the location of various historic sites and donated freely of his expertise in the preparation of the map outlining the boundaries of the "three Georges" which were combined to make the present city of Prince George.

David Richardson and the board and staff of the Fraser-Fort George Regional Museum deserve special praise for their cheerful, patient assistance and their willingness to make special arrangements to enable me to obtain copies of photographs from their collection, which are included in this book.

Photographer Lisa Murdoch also gave her time freely to ensure I had many of the photographs in this book.

I would also like to thank my daughter, Suzanne, who took many hours from her busy life to do research for the book at the Public Archives of B.C. in Victoria.

The staffs of the Prince George Public Library and the library of the College of New Caledonia also were continuously supportive and encouraging.

In the chapters that follow I have attempted to breathe some life into the history of Prince George. I hope, after reading it, you will view the community through new eyes and, when you look at particular landmarks such as The Cutbanks, Fort George Park, South Fort George, and what is now Spruceland subdivision, you will catch a glimmer of the hopes, dreams, disappointments, and courage of the people who were the pioneers of this city.

The Western-style shoes and shawl of this Indian woman carrying her baby were purchased with furs at Fort George. Courtesy, Provincial Archives of British Columbia

I

IN THE BEGINNING

An observer standing on Cranbrook Hill 10,000 to 12,000 years ago would have been standing on an island, staring across a vast triangular expanse of water stretching from Hixon in the south to Longworth in the east, Summit Lake in the north, and Bednesti Lake in the west—a huge lake which had been formed by the melting waters of the ice sheet which had previously covered the area. The released water was prevented from draining southward by an impervious barrier of lava and glacial debris.

But eventually the lake did drain, exposing the glacial debris and silt called outwash left by the lake which once covered much of the area now occupied by the older sections of the city of Prince George, reaching the level of the top of The Cutbanks. As the Nechako and Fraser rivers emerged, they began scouring their way down through the deposits of silt, sand, and fine gravel to reach bedrock which lay at the bottom of the lake.

It is thought that before the ice age several million years ago, the portion of the Fraser River north of Soda Creek was a tributary of the main body of the river which, instead of swinging around to flow south, flowed over the short piece of land which now separates the Fraser River from Summit Lake at Giscome Portage. From Summit Lake the water flowed via the Crooked, Parsnip, Peace, and Mackenzie rivers into the Arctic Ocean.

Evidence of the north-flowing Fraser can be found by examining modern maps of the area, which show that all the major tributaries of the Fraser River north of the mouth of the Chilcotin River begin by flowing northward, then suddenly change direction as they enter the larger river.

Geologists also point to the northerly slope of the gravel beds and benches deposited during the pre-glacial period as further evidence of the northward flow of the river during that time.

Near Soda Creek—which was the southward limit of steamboat travel in the early part of this century—the river enters a deep gorge. This is the point where the river broke through the barrier to initiate its southerly flow toward the Pacific Ocean.

Looking at the topography of the city today one can still see the benches of the ancient riverbeds. Such a riverbed can be found on the east side of Edmonton Street near Carney. To the north it continues past

A member of the Overlanders of 1862, en route to the gold fields near Barkerville, walks alongside the Fraser River. Watercolour by W.G.R. Hind. Courtesy, McCord Museum of Canadian History, McGill University, Montreal

the Prince George Regional Hospital toward Tenth Avenue. To the south the bank of this old riverbed swings past the north end of the Prince George Golf and Country Club to South Fort George. The banks of another riverbed can be found between First and Third avenues behind the government building, and South Fort George is built on a series of river-bottom terraces.

Remnants of the shoreline of the ancient lake can still be found today on the eastern shore of Tabor Lake, the sides of Cranbrook Hill, and near Haldi Lake. It has left a legacy in the form of soils—including the fine clay soils found in Pineview—which now nourish the evergreen forests covering the area and are the farming areas around Prince George.

CARRIER INDIANS ARRIVE

It is believed that central British Columbia's first residents, the Carrier Indians, followed migrating animals over the Bering Land Bridge from Asia more than 13,000 years ago. As the ice retreated, the Carrier Indians settled beside the lakes and rivers which were the remnants of the Ice Age. Here they found a ready supply of food in the form of wild animals, salmon migrating up the rivers, and trout and char occupying the lakes.

Prior to the arrival of the Europeans, the Carrier Indians clothed themselves in the skins and furs of the caribou, bears, beavers, marmots, and rabbits which they trapped. From these they fashioned robes, leggings, moccasins, mittens, and hats.

It is believed that moose did not move into the area until the late 1800s when, as a result of logging and land-clearing activities, the second-growth willows and aspen on which moose feed became more abundant.

Before the arrival of the Europeans, the Carrier Indians patterned their homes, tools, and weapons after those of neighboring tribes. Thus, in the south, they passed the winter in subterranean houses much like those used by the Chilcotin and Shuswap Indians, while in the north they spent the winter in multi-family lodges or longhouses much like those of the north coast Indians.

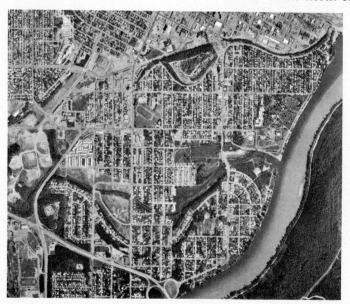

In this contemporary aerial photograph of Prince George, evidence of former river channels that were formed as the area drained are visible between Connaught Hill, centre, and South Fort George, lower right. Courtesy, Province of British Columbia

Bows and arrows, lances, clubs, and knives were the main weapons in the arsenal of these ancient residents of Prince George. To protect themselves in battle they fashioned body shields from slats of wood or thick animal hides.

The Carrier Indians also borrowed the potlatch system of the Haida and other north coast Indians. This complex system provided a form of public contract at a time when there were no written laws. Every social event of importance—the burial of a chief and the accession of a new one, the building of a new longhouse, a successful battle, the coming of age of a daughter or son, a marriage or funeral—was celebrated at a potlatch. Everyone attending the potlatch was a witness to the decisions and events occurring there and anyone who dared to break the public contract reached during a potlatch faced ostracism.

Like the Haida, the Carrier Indians acknowl-

*"Stoney Creek" Charlie was
photographed at Fort
George, circa 1910.
Courtesy, Provincial
Archives of British
Columbia*

edged a "supreme sky god" who was considered responsible for all
important events such as the migration of salmon, birth, and death. They
also believed all of nature was inhabited by supernatural beings. Sha-
mans or medicine men were also respected. It was believed they could
both inflict and heal disease and contact the supernatural spirits that
abounded in nature.

Prior to the arrival of Christian missionaries, the Carriers cremated
their dead. According to the present-day chief of the Fort George band,
Peter Quaw, his band's cremation ground was located on the bank of
the Nechako River near the junction of First Avenue and the Cameron
Street overpass.

It was from their practice of cremating their dead that the Carrier
Indians received their present-day name. According to the custom, a
widow was required to carry her husband's ashes and unburned bones

Left: This watercolour, by artist W.G.R. Hind, depicts the Overlanders travelling across the Rocky Mountains, through the Yellowhead Pass, circa 1862. Courtesy, McCord Museum of Canadian History, McGill University, Montreal

Circa 1862, artist W.G.R. Hind painted this Overlander pack mule beginning its descent into a steep valley. Courtesy, McCord Museum of Canadian History, McGill University, Montreal

Above: The Restless Scot, Alexander Mackenzie, was the first white man to travel through New Caledonia. In 1793 he led his crew of nine French Canadians across the Rocky Mountains in search of new fur-trading areas for the upstart North West Company. Courtesy, Provincial Archives of British Columbia

Right: When Simon Fraser died on August 18, 1862, he was buried among the Scots of Glengarry County at St. Andrews, in Eastern Ontario. Courtesy, Provincial Archives of British Columbia

in a pouch or basket on her back for as long as eight years. During this period she was a slave to her husband's family and, in most cases, could only be released from this bondage by the giving of a potlatch.

THE FIRST FUR TRADERS

Alexander Mackenzie was the first non-native to make the arduous trip across the Rocky Mountains into central B.C. In 1793 he used two Indians as interpreters and hunters to guide his crew of nine French Canadians and another Scot through the mountains in search of new fur-trading territory for the North West Company, which had sprung up in Montreal to challenge the monopoly of the British-based Hudson's Bay Company.

Although Mackenzie kept an extensive journal of his trip in which he noted the mouths of many local rivers and streams, he did not mention passing the mouth of the Nechako River.

It appears that June 19, 1793, was the day Mackenzie passed the confluence of what was then thought to be the Columbia and Nechako rivers. In his journal on that day he wrote only that ". . . there was an island, and it appeared to me, that the main channel of the river had formerly been on the other side of it."

This entry adds weight to the theory that Mackenzie did not see the mouth of the Nechako River because at that time the rivers were in flood and it entered the Fraser River on the west side of a large island which included Connaught Hill, and Mackenzie's canoe travelled along the eastern branch of the river.

On his return trip through the area on August 9, he again failed to mention the Nechako River. But, according to his journal, it was foggy when he and his men left their campsite at the north end of Fort George Canyon.

Although Mackenzie proved it was possible to cross the Rockies and

travel to the Pacific Ocean, it was 14 years before Simon Fraser constructed a permanent fort at the junction of what was then called The Great River and the Nechaco [sic] River in an area the Indians called Lheit-le, meaning the confluence of two rivers.

Fraser had passed through the area as he first paddled from Fort McLeod to Fort St. James, where he established the headquarters of the North West Company in 1806 in the territory he named New Caledonia. In 1807 Fort George became the fourth fort in Fraser's chain of trading posts in New Caledonia. On May 22, 1808, this fort was the launching point for his epic journey to the mouth of the tumultuous river that now bears his name. Fraser named Fort George in honor of King George III, who by then had been the king of Great Britain for 47 years of what was to be a 60-year reign.

When Fraser set out to explore The Great River in 1808, he left Hugh Faries in charge of Fort George. Little is known about Faries except that he had been posted at Rainy Lake, Ontario, in 1806 and, in 1816, was involved in a dispute between the Hudson's Bay Company and the North West Company near the headwaters of the Mississippi.

NEW CALEDONIA

As a result of the fur-trading activity of the North West Company in New Caledonia, Fort St. James was, until 1821, the seat of government in British Columbia. Following the union of the North West Company with the Hudson's Bay Company in 1821, the position of New Caledonia—and Fort George with it—began to change.

This Indian graveyard was once located on the land now occupied by Fort George Park. Courtesy, Provincial Archives of British Columbia

According to historian Walter Sage, after 1821 New Caledonia was viewed as the Siberia of the northwest fur-trading industry by George Simpson of the Hudson's Bay Company, for it was there he sent clerks he thought needed disciplining or with whom he was otherwise displeased. This behavior seemed contradictory since prior to 1821, Simpson had been actively planning to invade New Caledonia to gain control of the rich fur-bearing territory for the Hudson's Bay Company.

On February 22, 1822, the governor of the Hudson's Bay Company wrote to Simpson proposing they abandon the other Fort George on the Columbia River and concentrate their activities on trade in New Caledonia. In the same letter the governor also mentioned the Russians were claiming territory on the coast as far down as 51 degrees north latitude, near the northern tip of Vancouver Island.

In the letter the governor and his committee stated: "We think it is desirable to extend our trading posts as far to the west and north from the Fraser River in Caledonia as may be practicable, if there appears any reasonable prospect of doing it profitably."

How did early employees at isolated fur-trading posts such as those at Fort George spend their spare hours? According to Sage, fur-trading only occupied one-fifth of their time. Since most of them married or lived with native women and raised large families, a great deal of their time was taken up with domestic duties, including growing a garden, caring for poultry and other livestock, cutting firewood, and hunting and fishing for food. Most of the summer was taken up by the annual fur brigade to carry the bundles of fur to Hudson Bay via Winnipeg, and later to Fort Vancouver by canoe on the Columbia River.

There were occasional visits by Indians or officers from other posts, and these would be opportunities for dinner and a musical evening, or the telling of tales of dog races and hunting exploits or discussions of politics or religion. Long hours were also passed by playing chess and backgammon and, of course, writing long letters home. Time was also spent repairing structures and boats and building new ones.

Salmon—either fresh during the summer or dried during the winter—replaced pemmican as the staple food at the trading posts in New Caledonia. But an occasional change of diet was provided when hunters brought in a freshly killed deer or bear.

JAMES DOUGLAS

According to historian Father Adrien Morice, O.M.I., 1825 to 1830 was the most prosperous fur-trading period in New Caledonia. It was in 1825 that James Douglas, the man destined to become the first governor of the colonies of Vancouver Island and British Columbia, arrived in the area as a young clerk of the Hudson's Bay Company. It is known that in 1826 Douglas accompanied William Connolly, the chief factor of New Caledonia, and two Hudson's Bay clerks on the annual fur brigade, so it is likely he paid a visit to Fort George during that visit.

When he came to serve as a clerk at the Hudson's Bay Company post at Fort St. James, Douglas was told of the double murder that had occurred at Fort George in 1823. Although the deaths had taken place two years before he had even arrived at the fort, they resulted in a dramatic series of events which threatened Douglas' life and forced the young clerk's transfer from New Caledonia.

The murders were committed when James Murray Yale, the commander of Fort George, had left the fort to travel to Fort St. James to obtain more supplies. During his absence, the two men he had left in charge of the fort were stabbed to death and beheaded by their two Indian assistants, Tzill-na-o-lay and Un-la-yhin. According to historian Bruce McKelvie, the attack was provoked when one of the fur-traders reprimanded the Indians for their insolence during Yale's absence and threatened to report them to the commander on his return. Un-la-yhin fled over the Rocky Mountains into Alberta where he was killed by Cree Indians two years later; Tzill-na-o-lay disappeared.

Tzill-na-o-lay came out of hiding five years later, in the summer of 1828, when Chief 'Kwah, the ruler of the Carrier Indians, hosted a large gathering near Fort St. James.

Connolly had left Douglas, who was now his son-in-law, in charge of Fort St. James during his absence. Late one night an Indian informed Douglas that Tzill-na-o-lay had come into the Indian village for the feast and was hiding there. In the morning Douglas and several men began searching the village but, although they searched every house, they found nothing. However, the activities of one woman who had continued packing bundles as they searched had aroused Douglas' suspicions, so he returned to search that house a second time.

McKelvie describes the scene as follows: ". . . an arrow was thrust forward from the shadows. Douglas dodged, they plunged forward and seized the murderous Tzill-na-o-lay. A desperate struggle followed, only ending when one of the men struck the Indian on the head with a musket and felled him." Douglas reported the event to Connolly saying Tzill-na-o-lay had been "dispatched" in the Indian village "without confusion or any accident happening to any other individual."

Douglas should have known he was committing a grave insult to 'Kwah. By executing the murderer in the Indian village, he had involved 'Kwah in the act. According to Indian custom the chief was responsible for the safety of everyone in his village. When 'Kwah heard of the execution he became very angry. Two days later he and his warriors invaded and captured Fort St. James.

Douglas was bound hand and foot and, with one of 'Kwah's warriors holding a large dagger over his head, stood before the Indian chief awaiting the order for his death. But 'Kwah was reluctant to kill Douglas and instead demanded a ransom in the form of goods which he could use to compensate the dead man's relatives and restore his prestige. Eventually a deal was struck and Douglas and his men were released. But the matter was far from ended, for neither Tzill-na-o-lay's relatives nor the Hudson's Bay Company were prepared to forget the incident.

In the fall of 1828 George Simpson paid a ceremonial visit to the fort during which he scolded 'Kwah for capturing the fort and taking the employees captive. But Douglas intervened successfully on behalf of the Indian chief, explaining how the chief had spared his life.

Tzill-na-o-lay's relatives refused to accept 'Kwah's gifts as atonement for the death of their relative. But they did nothing to gain revenge until December 1828, when Douglas and a group of men set out to travel to Fort Fraser. When Douglas' party was in sight of the fort and crossing the Nautley River near the village of Natleh [sic], they were confronted by a group of 120 men from Noolah, a large Indian village near Vanderhoof. It was apparent the Indians intended to avenge the murder of their relative by capturing Douglas.

What happened next is recorded in the journal of Fort St. James for December 9, 1828:

Mr. Douglas relates a most atrocious attempt which was made against his life in passing through the village of Natleh [sic] on the 3d. inst., when he was surrounded by about 120 Indians, a great number of whom announced their intention of killing him and appeared fully prepared to perpetrate their infamous design, in which, however, they were prevented from succeeding, partly through the interference of Fraser's Lake Indians with Yazecho and some other well disposed people, but mostly by his own good and prudent conduct and the determination he evinced of selling his life dear should no other expedient be left of determining the affray.

Mr. Douglas with his three men faced them with presented arms and allowed them to exhaust their rage in threats, and did not quit the field until the rascals had all dispersed. This conduct was the most prudent he could have followed, for if he had retreated towards the post (about two miles distant from the spot where this scene was exhibited) he would no doubt have been followed thither by all the villans by whom he was assaulted, and the affair would not have terminated without bloodshed.

The blame for the incident was placed on the Indians of Noolah and Thluchleh, which was a village on the Nechako River near Fort George.

Because the incident remained unresolved, Douglas' life was constantly threatened. As a result, on February 27, 1829, Connolly recommended that Douglas be transferred out of the area. He was sent to the Columbia District, where he caught the eye of company officials and quickly advanced to become commander of the district and governor of the Colony of British Columbia.

This young Indian woman was photographed at Fort George in 1910. Courtesy, Provincial Archives of British Columbia

Thomas McMicking was the chosen leader of the Overlanders who arrived at Fort George on September 6, 1862. Courtesy, Provincial Archives of British Columbia

II

THE SETTLERS ARRIVE

During its first 100 years Fort George slumbered in the wilderness while two other central-interior British Columbia communities, Fort St. James and Quesnel, were drawn into the historical spotlight.

Fort St. James reigned as the capital of New Caledonia during the early part of the nineteenth century, when the North West Company's fur empire dominated trade in the area. In the 1860s, when gold was discovered on Antler Creek southeast of Barkerville, Quesnel flared into prominence as the main trading post of the interior.

After amalgamating with the North West Company in 1821, the Hudson's Bay Company had difficulty supplying its inland trading posts in New Caledonia. Four main trading routes were used to carry supplies into the area.

In the beginning they used the Peace-Parsnip River route by which Alexander Mackenzie and Simon Fraser had made their way into the area. In 1807 Fraser shortened the route by building an 83-mile trail connecting Fort St. James and Fort McLeod.

In 1825 John Stuart, the man who had accompanied Fraser on his heroic journey to the mouth of the Fraser River, opened a new route into New Caledonia which followed the Stuart, Nechako, and Fraser rivers downstream to Fort Alexandria. From there pack horses were used to transport goods to Fort Thompson (Kamloops), and then to Fort Okanagan on the Columbia River, where the goods were loaded into canoes and taken to Fort Vancouver.

In 1846, when the Oregon Treaty ceded the lower Columbia River to the United States, it became necessary to develop a new route into New Caledonia to avoid having to pay American tariffs. The Hudson's Bay Company abandoned Fort Vancouver and established Fort Langley 30 miles up the Fraser River, and located an alternate route to New Caledonia which followed the Fraser River to its junction with the Coquihalla River. From there a pack-horse trail led along the Coquihalla River Valley to its junction with the old route at Fort Thompson on the Thompson River.

Another route out of New Caledonia led up the Fraser from Fort

George and through the Yellowhead Pass onto the prairies. The Europeans called this route the Leather Pass, because over it Indians and traders carried the supplies of caribou and moose hides used to make moccasins, leather thongs, and clothing. Today known as the Yellowhead, it is believed that the pass was named after a blond Indian who had a cache at the foot of the pass.

THE OVERLANDERS

It was from Tête Jaune Cache in 1862 that an expedition began which would result in the tragic deaths of four men on the turbulent waters of the Fraser River's Grand Canyon, 100 miles upstream from Fort George.

A group of more than 150 people, now known as the Overlanders, had set out from Eastern Canada to travel 3,500 miles overland to make their fortune in the gold fields in the Cariboo region of B.C. When the poorly equipped party finally made its way across the Rocky Mountains and came down to the Fraser River near Tête Jaune Cache, they had nearly run out of supplies. A story is told of one member of the party who became so hungry he stewed his deerskin tumpline and ate it. Others killed their starving oxen and horses for food or foraged for whatever they could find in the wilderness.

Some of the Overlanders decided to continue their journey by finding the trail that the Indians said would lead them down the North Thompson River. But the majority of the gold-seekers, including Thomas McMicking, the leader of the main party, thought the Fraser River offered an easier route to Quesnel.

It was late August and the temperature at night was already dropping to near freezing, so the men set to work at once, constructing the huge rafts on which they planned to float down the Fraser River. William Sellar was in charge of the largest raft, reported by historian Mark Wade to have been 85 feet long. On the first half of the craft were placed nine head of oxen, while the passengers and their supplies were confined to the rear. Other Overlanders exchanged horses for canoes to make the trip down the river. One man made a boat from a framework of saplings over which he stretched untanned ox hides.

On September 1, 1862, the strange flotilla left Tête Jaune Cache. For the first four days, the travellers rested as the river bore them along. Meals were cooked and served on the rafts and, unaware of the dangers of the river, they even slept on the drifting craft.

But all was not perfect. Thomas McMicking reported in his journal that the weather was very wet, cold, and uncomfortable throughout the river journey. John Hunniford wrote in his diary: "Rainy all day, very uncomfortable, diarrhoea very bad on board, meat badly tainted—our flour about done."

On September 5 the cumbersome rafts passed safely through several rapids before entering the Grand Canyon, at the foot of which there is a whirlpool. Historian Margaret McNaughton described the scene as one

On December 1, 1910, while exploring the Lower Canyon of the Nechako River, these men posed for a photograph. A hollowed-out cottonwood tree, in a style used by the Indians, is their mode of transportation. Courtesy, Provincial Archives of British Columbia.

raft was drawn into the vortex of swirling water: "The men clung to the raft; the animals fortunately were tied to the railing. Round and round the craft whirled. At the first plunge those on the shore could see only the horns of the oxen, but the raft being very wide, the suction was not great enough to submerge it entirely."

Despite the danger, all the rafts made their way through the boiling rapids and drifted into calmer waters. Those who were travelling in canoes, however, were less fortunate.

Arthur Robertson, Robert Warren, and a man identified only as Douglas had been riding in two canoes that were lashed together. The cumbersome craft capsized and broke apart when it entered the canyon, and the three occupants were thrown into the icy water. Robertson, who was an expert swimmer, ordered Douglas and Warren to cling to the canoe as he set off to swim to shore. As they struggled to keep their heads above water, the two men observed Robertson swimming strongly toward the shore. But, when they looked back after the current of the river had carried them to the safety of a small island, Robertson had disappeared beneath the water. His body was never found. Douglas and Warren were rescued by two members of the crew of the Huntingdon raft, William Sellar and Alexander Fortune, who launched a canoe from the raft and paddled to the aid of the exhausted, half-frozen men.

The canoe bearing Eustace Pattison, William Mackenzie, and a man identified only as Carrol had left Tête Jaune Cache first and arrived at the Grand Canyon ahead of the slower-moving rafts. When they saw how dangerous the canyon was, they attempted to use a rope to guide their canoe through the rapids. But it quickly filled with water and sank, carrying all their supplies with it.

Pattison had already been ill with a sore throat when he and his party were forced to spend two uncomfortable days waiting to be rescued, exposed to incessant rain and without food. By the time the bedraggled travellers floated onto the river bank below Fort George on September 6, Pattison was gravely ill. In spite of the care given him by another member of the party, Dr. Edward Stevenson, he died that night. As there were no boards available to make a coffin, Pattison's body was placed in half of a small canoe. The other half of the canoe was lashed over him before he was buried near the southern end of what is now Fort George Park.

According to McMicking's journals, Eustace Pattison was 19 at the time of his death. He was a shy, quiet young man, and a "keen student of biology." Born at Launceston, Cornwall, England, he was the son of Samuel Rowles Pattison, a London solicitor. Eustace Pattison was also the first white man known to have been buried at Fort George. The exact location of his grave is unknown.

Two other men are known to have died at the canyon: James Carpenter, a barrister from Toronto, and Phillip Leader of Huron, Ontario, who drowned when his canoe capsized as he tried to make his way through the Grand Canyon.

Carpenter had explored the length of the canyon before attempting to navigate it. He appeared to have foreseen his death, for afterwards his companions found a note in the pocket of a jacket he had left behind. It read: "Arrived this day at the cañon [sic] at 10 P.M. and drowned running the canoe down. God keep my poor wife." Carpenter was reported to have been weak from scurvy. He had been unable to eat the pemmican which was the only food they had been able to obtain for the last part of the trip. Instead, he had been forced to survive on flour and water.

Carpenter was not the only white man who found it impossible to eat pemmican, made from dried, lean meat which had been pounded into a coarse powder. Sometimes dry berries were added. The mixture was packed into a bag made of animal hide before melted tallow was poured over the contents to seal it. In his journals, Hudson's Bay Company governor George Simpson described its consistency, taste, and appearance in these words: "Take the scrapings from the driest outside corner of a very stale piece of cold roast beef, add to it lumps of tallowy, rancid fat, then garnish that with long human hairs on which are strung pieces like beads upon a necklace and the short hairs of dogs or oxen or both and you have a fair imitation of common pemmican."

The surviving members of the group arrived at Fort George in an emaciated condition after having only a small supply of dried mountain

sheep, a little tea, and a few berries to eat during the five-day trip. They rested in Fort George for two days, awaiting the return of the chief trader, William Charles, who was on a trip to Quesnel to obtain supplies.

Margaret McNaughton reported that on the third day they could wait no longer for the return of the chief trader. After obtaining potatoes, turnips, berries, and bear, beaver, and badger meat from the Indians living near the fort, they followed some Indian guides through Fort George Canyon, 15 miles down the river from the fort; pushed away from the shore; and resumed their perilous journey.

This time everyone made it safely through both the Fort George and Cottonwood canyons. Later that day, when they saw miners working beside the river, they knew they had finally reached the Fraser River gold fields.

The group disbanded at Quesnel. According to historian Mark Wade, few of them found their fortunes in the gold fields, but one, John Bowron, became gold commissioner and government agent and left his name on a lake and river in the area.

HISTORY BY-PASSES FORT GEORGE

Throughout the rest of the nineteenth century fortune continued to ignore Fort George. When the colony of B.C. spent a million dollars between 1862 and 1865 building the Cariboo Wagon Road, it followed a route along the Fraser River to Quesnel, then turned eastward to carry supplies to the miners who were scouring the gold-bearing creeks in the mountains near Barkerville.

In 1865, when the ill-fated Collins Overland Telegraph Line was built in an unsuccessful attempt to carry telegraph lines through B.C. to Europe via the Yukon, Alaska, Siberia, and Russia, it too by-passed Fort George by following the Blackwater Trail from Quesnel to the point where it crossed the Blackwater (West Road) River. From there the Telegraph Trail continued northwestward into northern B.C. via Hazelton.

Two surges of gold miners used the Telegraph Trail to by-pass Fort George: the miners who had joined the Omineca Gold Rush into the

Above: As freight scow traffic increased on the Fraser River between Tête Jaune Cache and Fort George, a portage for horses was built and used to transport cargo safely around the Grand Canyon. Courtesy, Fraser-Fort George Regional Museum

area north of Fort St. James in 1871 and, in 1898, a northern surge of miners who had moved over the trail on their way to the Klondike.

Throughout this period the route into Fort George beyond the Blackwater River was marked only by a rough track. But that changed when, in July 1903, an agreement was signed between the federal government and the Grand Trunk Pacific Railway Company to construct a railway line from Winnipeg through central B.C. to the Pacific Ocean at the port of Prince Rupert. Rumors that as many as 19 railways would crisscross the valley at the junction of the Fraser and Nechako rivers signalled a rush of people into Fort George over the Blackwater Trail. Most of these early settlers hoped to make their fortune by buying or pre-empting land in the area while it was still cheap, and either subdividing it and selling it or establishing farms to supply the large city that was expected to spring up there.

Settlers arriving at the fort in the early 1900s reported travelling along the Cariboo Wagon Road to Quesnel where they either swam the Fraser River or crossed by ferry, then travelled over the Blackwater Trail on foot or horseback. Dog teams were used to travel the route during the winter when frozen rivers and Indian trails served as a highway. As the railway construction progressed, supplies were brought down the Fraser River to Fort George from Tête Jaune Cache. By 1912, more than 100 scows a day were reported to be leaving Tête Jaune Cache carrying supplies for the construction workers and settlers crowding into the area around Fort George. It is reported that in one season more than 70 of the men working on those scows met their deaths in the same canyon that had claimed the lives of the four Overlanders.

Later, a pack-horse trail was built around the canyon to prevent the loss of lives and supplies in that dangerous portion of the river. In the winter, horse-drawn sleds were used to carry supplies along the rivers and rough roads. As the rush of settlers grew, stern-wheelers began plying the Fraser River above Soda Creek.

Right: A train of pack horses crosses the bridge at Blackwater River. This was the first road built north of Quesnel for the purpose of transporting supplies to Vanderhoof and points west. Courtesy, Provincial Archives of British Columbia

STERN-WHEELERS PLY THE RIVERS

The first stern-wheeler, the *Nechacco*, nudged its keel against the shallow banks of the Fraser River near South Fort George in 1909. Soon the big boats were making their way along the river from Soda Creek to Tête Jaune Cache and west along the Nechako River. The sight and sound of these shallow-draft vessels huffing and puffing their way toward the community must have filled the residents with awe.

In his memoirs, the late Wiggs O'Neill, who was a part owner of the *Inlander*, the last paddle-wheeler on the Skeena River, described the deep bay of the stern-wheeler's whistle and the "slap-slap-slap" of the paddles hitting the water. He also left this colorful description of the sight of a stern-wheeler making its way upstream: "To me, a stern-wheeler slapping her way through the white-water rapids, spray cascading from the bow and paddle-wheel, steam and smoke belching skyward in great swirls of black and white was a picture that, once seen, was never forgotten."

There are records of 12 stern-wheelers having plied the waters of the Upper Fraser and Nechako rivers during the early part of this century: the *Enterprise, Victoria, Charlotte, Nechacco* (renamed the *Chilco*), *Quesnel, Fort Fraser* (renamed the *Doctor*), *B.C. Express, Chilcotin, Operator, Conveyor, Robert C. Hammond,* and *BX*—the queen of the stern-wheelers landing at Fort George. Despite the superstitions surrounding her launching date of Friday, May 13, 1910, the *BX* was the first stern-wheeler to succeed in establishing a twice-a-week schedule between Soda Creek and Fort George.

Although the owners of smaller boats sailing between Soda Creek and Fort George predicted the *BX*'s broader beam would prevent her from navigating the tight turns in the canyons, she became the first stern-wheeler to navigate the Fort George and Cottonwood canyons under her own steam. Until then, all the stern-wheelers had used land lines to stabilize them as they made their way through Fort George Canyon where the river splits into three channels and surges around rocky barriers.

The 50-year history of the stern-wheelers that navigated the Upper Fraser between 1871 and 1921 is punctuated by colorful stories of accidents. In his book, *Paddlewheels on the Frontier*, historian Art Downs reported that on one trip over the seven-mile-long Giscome Rapids, the stern-wheeler *Quesnel* had 15 holes punched in her hull. According to Downs: "These holes were repaired with a 'soft patch'—usually a wad of oakum slapped on the hole and held in place by a post wedged against the deck. If there was no oakum, sacks of flour or anything soft was substituted. Many a side of bacon became a temporary hull patch rather than a companion for breakfast eggs."

The first stern-wheelers were more practical than luxurious.

Top: On May 1, 1910, the first white women arrived at South Fort George. Courtesy, Fraser-Fort George Regional Museum

Above: The "Queen of the Upper Fraser," the BX, *could carry 120 passengers in 70 steam-heated staterooms. It was the first stern-wheeler to establish a biweekly schedule between Soda Creek and Fort George. Courtesy, Fraser-Fort George Regional Museum*

Passengers aboard the stern-wheeler Charlotte *assist in loading cords of wood; fuel necessary to reach its destination via the Fraser River. Courtesy, Fraser-Fort George Regional Museum*

Passengers were asked to bring their own blankets so they could roll up in them and sleep on the deck. They were also called upon to help with the chores involved in the operation of the vessels, such as loading the cords of wood used to provide the steam or lining the vessels through the more treacherous rapids and canyons.

But when the *BX* was launched at Soda Creek she provided a more luxurious style of accommodation for her 130 passengers. The ship's 70 steam-heated staterooms were furnished with velvet carpets and thick mattresses. The tables in the dining room were set with English china and monogrammed linen and silverware. To add to the passengers' comfort, there were bathrooms with hot and cold running water and a staff of Japanese servants to attend to the travellers' needs.

SETTLEMENT BEGINS AT SOUTH FORT GEORGE

When the building boom got under way in South Fort George in 1910 there were six stern-wheelers carrying freight and passengers to the town. In 1909 the first sawmill had been built in the community by the Fort George Lumber and Navigation Company, owned by Nick Clark. Demand for lumber was so great buyers were hauling the boards away as they came off the saw. The following year two more sawmills began turning out lumber for the growing community. One, owned by Russell Peden and William Cooke, was located near Peden Hill. The other had been built by the Natural Resources Security Company which was developing the land near the Nechako River—later the townsite of Central Fort George.

Another source of lumber was the large wooden freight scows making their way down the river from Tête Jaune Cache. After they arrived at Fort George the scows were sold for salvage. The river men would then buy or make a canoe—usually from a hollowed-out cottonwood tree—in which they would pole their way back up the river to Tête Jaune Cache, where they would build another scow to carry another load of freight downstream. One of the best-known of these early scowmen was George Williams, who later established a store in South Fort George. When Prince George became the centre of development, he moved his store to Third Avenue in the building now occupied by W.D. West Studios.

By the summer of 1909 there were three general stores operating in South Fort George—the Hudson's Bay Company store near the Indian reserve, William Blair and Company on the 97 acres south of the Indian reserve owned by Alexander G. Hamilton, and Hamilton's store—and a barbershop owned by Frank Hoferkamp, located on Joseph Lapage's preemption. Tent-covered shacks served as the offices of the area's first bank and newspaper.

In the spring of 1910 Lorne MacHaffie, John "Jock" Munro, and J. Anderson disguised themselves as prospectors as a means of preventing robberies when they carried $50,000 into the fort over the Blackwater

Trail. The money was used to open the Bank of British North America in a building with a canvas roof and wooden sides and floor.

John Houston was the publisher of the first newspaper, the *Fort George Tribune*. The first edition was published on November 6, 1909. As there were few people to subscribe to the newspaper, it served primarily to inform prospective settlers and investors of the opportunities in the new community. Because the law required the publication of notices of all lands staked, and the land boom was just beginning in New Caledonia, legal notices were the tiny newspaper's main source of income.

In the edition of the paper printed November 20, 1909, in answer to questions from readers about the conditions at Fort George, editor Houston replied:

There are no women and no place for women to stop at. Men can get a meal at two places where they can sleep if they have their own blankets. Fort George is a Hudson's Bay Company store and an Indian village of 100 men, women and children. South Fort George is where the town is at present . . . A boarding-house well kept and with white people as cooks and waiters would be a Godsend to any man of the Cariboo. There are no bakeries, laundries, milliners, tailors, blacksmiths, tinners, carpenters, stenographers, lawyers, doctors, preachers, constables or school teachers in Fort George. There are no white children or women to raise white children.

J.A.F. "Doc" Campbell, who came to South Fort George in 1908 with a survey crew, said at that time there were three residents: a Hudson's Bay Company factor, a farmer, and a Northwest Mounted Policeman who made a living selling a mixture of "tobacco juice and cayenne pepper" as whiskey.

Above: John Houston, left, of the Fort George Tribune, *the first newspaper published in Prince George, stands before the tent-roofed shack that served as the city's first newspaper office. Courtesy, The Citizen*

Left: Lorne MacHaffie, manager, John "Jock" Munro, and J. Anderson disguised themselves as prospectors to confuse potential robbers when they carried $50,000 into South Fort George to open the first bank. Courtesy, Provincial Archives of British Columbia

John McInnis, who arrived by horse-drawn sleigh in 1910, reported timber was growing on the townsite of South Fort George, which was then nothing more than a collection of tents. There were fewer than a dozen white men and no white women "closer than Quesnel" when he came to the area. Pioneer Pineview farmer Ernie Pinker described the construction of an ice bridge across the Fraser River during the winter, facilitating travel to South Fort George.

By December 1910 Alexander G. Hamilton was operating a stagecoach from South Fort George to Quesnel on the first and third Monday of each month, returning on the following Saturday. Depending on the conditions the trip took four or five days.

Although Houston reported that letters of enquiry about the prospects in the new community arrived in every mail, there were still relatively few people residing there. On November 11, 1909, the *Fort George Tribune* reported there were 100 Indians, the manager of the Hudson's Bay Company store, and the manager's cook living on the Fort George reserve. About 20 white men lived half a mile away, at South Fort George. The paper reported that "there were 75 pre-emptors and 15 more in the Fraser River valley between Fort George and Giscombe Portage."

Late that year Nick Clark, owner of the Fort George Lumber and Navigation Company, announced his plans to install a small lighting plant and water system in South Fort George in the spring of 1910 to service the hotel he would be building there.

On May 1, 1910, the first white women arrived in the community. The *Vancouver Province* of May 7, 1910, reported only that they were the wives of C. House, Hallam, and Teamaher. A photograph taken upon their arrival shows several small children accompanied them but their names are not given. The Vancouver newspaper said only that ". . . Teamaher will remain in town and the other two go with their families to pre-emption holdings up the Nechaco [sic]."

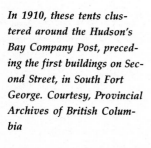

In 1910, these tents clustered around the Hudson's Bay Company Post, preceding the first buildings on Second Street, in South Fort George. Courtesy, Provincial Archives of British Columbia

*Above: Nick Clark's saw-
mill on the bank of the
Nechako River supplied the
lumber for the first buildings in South Fort George.
When the sawmill was built
in 1909, the demand for
lumber was so great that buyers were hauling the boards
away as they emerged from
the saw. Courtesy, Provincial Archives of British
Columbia*

In 1807, Simon Fraser named Fort George in honor of King George III, seen here. Since 1915, when the city of Prince George was incorporated, there has existed an ongoing dispute regarding which member of British royalty was meant to be honored when the new name, Prince George, was chosen. Portrait by Allan Ramsey, circa 1762.
Courtesy, Public Archives of Canada

III

A TALE OF THREE GEORGES

W hen Prince George was incorporated as a city on March 6, 1915, it included all the land between the Fraser River on the east, the Nechako River on the north, Fraser Street (now known as Carney Street) on the west, and Bowser Street (now known as 17th Avenue) on the south.

The city was incorporated during a bitter fight over the location of a railway station in which the Grand Trunk Pacific Railway Company claimed the right to decide where the station should be, and George Hammond, the flamboyant spokesman for the Natural Resources Security Company, claimed he had an agreement with the railway company to place the station on or adjacent to his property at the west end of First Avenue.

The Grand Trunk Pacific Railway's application to the federal government in 1908 to purchase land in the vicinity of the Hudson's Bay Company trading post, which it planned to use as its railway yard, resulted in lengthy negotiations between the railway company, the Department of Indian Affairs, the governent of Canada, and the Province of B.C. This gave Hammond time to gain control of the flat bench of land west of the Indian reserve, where he predicted the railway station would be built. Soon the Natural Resources Security Company had embarked on a worldwide, half-million-dollar sales campaign to sell lots in its new townsite. Throughout the early part of this sales campaign Hammond claimed that the railway station would be located on his townsite. When it later became apparent the railway company had no intention of locating its station on the townsite, Hammond began fighting to have the station located close to the townsite's eastern boundary, near the present-day Cameron Street overpass.

Meanwhile, the railway company began negotiating with the Fort George Indian band for possession of its 1,366-acre reserve at the junction of the Fraser and Nechako rivers, but this proved to be time-consuming because it was necessary to negotiate with the Department of Indian Affairs instead of directly with the Fort George tribe.

Charles Millar, owner of the B.C. Express Company, also recognized the value of the property and sent his agent to begin negotiating with

Above: Father Coccola, left, joins two Indians, and another hunter, as they examine a recently shot deer. Courtesy, Fraser-Fort George Regional Museum

Below: The office of the Natural Resources Security Co. Ltd. was the scene of considerable activity during the selling of lots in Fort George. Men from around the world gathered outside the company office on Central Street to read the lists of lots for sale in the community being touted as the "next Chicago." Courtesy, Fraser-Fort George Regional Museum

the Indians through their spokesman, Father Nicolas Coccola. When Millar's agent approached Coccola with a telegram from the Department of Indian Affairs, Coccola believed Millar had the department's sanction and made arrangements to sell the land to him. But the Grand Trunk Pacific intervened and convinced the department to cancel the sale by saying Millar's agent was not authorized to finalize the purchase. That done, the railway company acted quickly to purchase the land through Father Coccola for $125,000 in 1913.

This time Millar went to court claiming his agreement of sale was legitimate. The railway company then agreed to give Millar 200 acres on the southeastern corner of their townsite. He subdivided the property, which became known as the Millar Addition, and put it on the market in 1914. Millar gained national fame in the 1940s when he initiated what came to be known as a "stork derby" by leaving a portion of his estate to the Ontario woman who bore the most children during the 10 years following his death.

HAMMOND'S AMBITIOUS PLANS

It was George Hammond's struggle to have the railway station located near his townsite that developed into a most bitter battle. Even by today's standards, Hammonds' plans for the development of Central Fort George would be considered a bold undertaking. And, when considering that he was promoting a piece of property in the wilderness with no amenities and only the promise of a railway to provide an all-weather route into the area, his plans assume superhuman proportions.

But the remoteness of the property did not daunt Hammond, and by 1912 he had amassed an interest in more than 2,000 acres in Central Fort George and divided them into 20,000 lots. According to a research essay completed by Anna Bumby in 1981, neither Hammond nor his company owned the property that they were offering for sale in the townsite they had officially registered as Fort George. (The choice of the name ignored the fact that the historical name of Fort George had been given to the area around the old Hudson's Bay trading post 2.3 miles away on the banks of another river.) According to Bumby, throughout his colorful association with Fort George, Hammond was acting only as a selling agent for the owners of the property.

For example, in the case of District Lots 937 and 938, the owners of the land, John Hugo Ross of Winnipeg and George Barbey of Paris, France, entered into an agreement whereby they sold 6 to 12 lots at a time to William Campbell of Winnipeg for one dollar each. Campbell would then sell the lots to Hammond's company for approximately $75 each, and by January 1913 Hammond was selling the same lots for $500 to $1,000 each.

Bumby reveals that Hammond made similar sales arrangements with Pacific Securities of Nelson, B.C., which owned 890 lots in District Lot

The topographical survey crew who laid the groundwork for the city of Prince George, posed for this photograph while in camp on payday. From left to right are: Hicks, Anderson, Vaughan, Hall, Billman, McDonald, McCann, and Sparks. The name of the man in the second row has been excluded. Courtesy, Fraser-Fort George Regional Museum

Smoke identifies the location of the sawmill in South Fort George, viewed from the west bank of the Fraser River in 1910. The Indian village and the Hudson's Bay Trading Post can be seen just beyond the trees. Courtesy, Provincial Archives of British Columbia

By 1913, the land boom was under way, and South Fort George had taken on a more settled appearance. Courtesy, Provincial Archives of British Columbia

The Grand Trunk Pacific Railway was opposed to George Hammond's bold plan for the development of Central Fort George. Courtesy, Fraser-Fort George Regional Museum

Below: In 1911, Central Avenue looked less than well settled; however, George Hammond was sending out brochures which advertised the amenities to be found in the Fort George townsite at that time. Courtesy, Fraser-Fort George Regional Museum

1429, and with two Vancouver businessmen, James Hillis and Elliot Haswell, regarding District Lot 777.

The significant factor in all of these deals was that neither Hammond nor the Natural Resources Security Company appeared to have had any money invested in the property they were advertising for sale at the Fort George townsite. Furthermore, in the case of Pacific Securities, the agreement's schedule of payments specified that if Hammond was unable to sell enough lots before November 1912, he lost everything.

In an effort to meet these deadlines, Hammond embarked on an ambitious international advertising campaign designed to appeal to the world-wide interest in cheap land and publicize the opportunities in the new frontiers opening up in Western Canada.

According to the July 1, 1910, edition of the Vancouver newspaper *The Saturday Sunset*, the first sale of lots was an outstanding success. It reported: ". . . the rush to secure property in this portion of the coming central British Columbian city was so rapid that the property was over-sold by eight hundred lots in little over two months."

Examining Hammond's advertising material today, it is obvious he was prepared to do anything—including stretching the truth—to convince people they should invest their money in his townsite. Samples of the flowery rhetoric contained in some of this early advertising material include:

The Nechacco [sic] and the Stuart link up a series of splendid lakes that together form a chain of communication unequalled anywhere on the continent except by the Great Lakes and the St. Lawrence . . .

Eleven railways are either chartered or building into this region, and every one of them touches Fort George . . .

The great region contains, according to evidence given before the Senate of the Dominion of Canada, 60,000,000 acres, and of this immense area 40,000,000 acres is reported as first class agricultural land . . .

The brochures also contained statements comparing Fort George to Winnipeg and Chicago, as the transportation hub through which "every bushel of grain, every hoof of stock, every pound of merchandise raised or required for a territory one-third the area of the whole of Europe must go or come."

Another brochure contained a map showing the Fort George business centre, including a station and post office located at the centre of a bull's-eye on Hammond's property. But photographs taken at the time indicate the townsite of Fort George fell far short of Hammond's optimistic descriptions and, in fact, consisted of nothing more than a few small buildings surrounded by acres of stumps. Hammond appeared to have realized Fort George must have a more developed appearance if he was going to be successful in promoting it as the site of a future city. So he began constructing the necessary permanent buildings himself.

By 1910 the Natural Resources Security Company had built the Hotel Fort George near the north end of Central Avenue. Fort George Hall and the public library were located in a small building provided by the company. Hammond personally donated a lot and a manse for the Presbyterian church and the Natural Resources Security Company provided two lots for a Methodist church.

In 1910 Hammond also succeeded in badgering the federal government into establishing a post office for the community in a building provided by the company. Since there was already a post office in South Fort George, the addition of another with a similar name within three miles created much confusion in the delivery of the mail.

But Hammond's far-reaching advertising campaign appears to have also benefited the landowners in South Fort George. According to *A History of Prince George* by Rev. Francis Edwin Runnalls, by 1913, before there were any permanent residents living in Prince George, there were 1,000 people in Fort George and 1,200 in South Fort George.

FAILURE FOLLOWS SUCCESS

In 1911 Hammond met with Winnipeg financier John Hugo Ross and Grand Trunk Pacific president Charles Hays and convinced them of the

Below: During the brisk sale of the first lots on the Fort George townsite, the auctioneer stood on a balcony of the Hotel Fort George. Courtesy, Fraser-Fort George Regional Museum

potential for development at Fort George. At the time, proposals were being considered for 10 railways, including the Grand Trunk Pacific and the Pacific Great Eastern (PGE), which would intersect near Hammond's townsite. Later Hammond claimed he had reached an unwritten "gentleman's agreement" with Hays at this meeting, in which Hays agreed to locate the Grand Trunk Pacific station at the west end of First Avenue for $250,000.

Hammond's plans seemed to be coming together in 1912 when the Conservative provincial government of Richard McBride gave approval for the building of the PGE from Vancouver to the Peace River. But they began to fall apart later that year when, on April 12, Hays and Ross were drowned dur-

Left: This group of early settlers in Fort George gathered outside the offices of the Natural Resources Security Co. Ltd. on the day the first automobile arrived aboard a stern-wheeler. Courtesy, Provincial Archives of British Columbia

Above: Smoldering ruins were all that remained of the Hotel Fort George after a fire swept through an entire block of the city. Courtesy, Fraser-Fort George Regional Museum

Prince George's first railway station, built near the north end of George Street, was used until a permanent station was constructed in 1922. Courtesy, Provincial Archives of British Columbia

ing the sinking of the *Titanic.* Hays' successor, Edson Chamberlin, refused to honor Hays' commitment to place the station close to the boundary of the Fort George townsite.

Hammond's troubles increased when the Toronto-based publication *Saturday Night* began publishing a series of articles exposing Hammond's questionable advertising campaign to promote the sale of lots in Fort George. Hammond immediately sought an injunction to prevent the magazine from publishing any more of the damaging articles.

But the judge denied Hammond's application for the injunction, saying the Natural Resources Security Company had published a series of brochures which included maps showing the Grand Trunk Pacific station as being located in Fort George when, in fact, the site of the station had not yet been determined. Hammond then tried to restore his credibility by offering the railway company $200,000 for a commitment to locate the station within 1,320 feet of the eastern boundary of Fort George.

The death blow to Hammond's plans was struck on Friday the 13th of November 1914, when an early-morning fire raged down Central Avenue, destroying 2 hotels and 11 stores. The fire started in the Hotel Fort George, and when the ashes cooled the only person unaccounted for was the occupant of Room 10, Richard Spence of Spokane, Washington, an engineer employed by the contracting firm of H.E. Carleton and Co.

Following Hays' death the Grand Trunk Pacific Railway began a determined effort to build a station at the eastern end of First Avenue where it could provide better service to the Hudson's Bay Company trading post and South Fort George. To prevent the railway company from acting without considering the wishes of the local residents, the federal government stepped into the fight, ruling that railway officials needed to have the Board of Railway Commissioners of Canada approve the location of the station. Hammond appeared before the board in 1912 in an effort to have them enforce his agreement with Hays to have the station located at the west end of what is now First Avenue, but he succeeded only in obtaining a ruling prohibiting the railway company from locating its station at the other end of First Avenue.

Peter Wilson and N.E. Montgomery represented the property owners of Prince George and South Fort George during the railway commission hearings. They joined the railway company in advocating that the station be located near the eastern end of First Avenue. In 1915, in an attempt to overthrow the board's decision to locate the station 2,700 feet west of George Street, Wilson and Montgomery circulated a citizens' petition which had been drafted by the railway company's lawyer. It was necessary to maintain the appearance that the railway company was not involved in the petition because

it could not contest the decision without appearing to be acting in default of the board's order.

Although the citizens' petition succeeded in delaying a final decision by the board, it became apparent that only the incorporation of a city would give local citizens the power they needed to have the station built adjacent to most of the community's businesses, which were now located on George Street.

The railway company continued to stall by dragging the dispute through four more hearings of the Board of Railway Commissioners of Canada plus an appeal to the governor-in-council before it was finally quashed in March 1921. The final hearing determined the station should be built two blocks west of George Street between Quebec and Dominion streets.

By that time most of the businessmen who had purchased property in Fort George realized Hammond was losing the fight to have the station built near his townsite and either moved their buildings into Prince George or abandoned their property and rebuilt in the new townsite.

Despite below-zero temperatures, the rail line across the Fraser River was completed on January 27, 1914, and the first train to cross the river pulled up beside the temporary station and freight sheds at the end of George Street. This station was used until the permanent station was built between Quebec and Dominion streets in 1922.

The Grand Trunk Pacific Railway Company's influence over the formation of the city extended further than the location of its station. It also exercised considerable influence over the name chosen for the new city, the design of the city's streets, and the formation of the city's first municipal council.

For example, in 1912, long before the dispute over the location of the station had been settled, the railway company spent $6 million commissioning a Boston firm of landscape architects, Brett, Hall and Co., to design the street layout for the new townsite of Prince George. An examination of those plans reveals the company obviously intended the city hall to be located on Princess Square at the south end of George Street, and the railway station was to have been the focal point of an impressive square at the north end of George Street into which led George, Edson, and Morley streets and First Avenue.

Peter Wilson represented the property owners of Prince George during the railway commission hearings which determined the site of the Grand Trunk Pacific Railway station. Courtesy, Jane Kennedy

Top: Within six weeks time more than eight buildings had been constructed on George Street, the main thoroughfare of the new "boom" town. Courtesy, Fraser-Fort George Regional Museum

Above: By September 1914, George Street was lined with buildings and the Hotel Prince George was nearing completion. Courtesy, Fraser-Fort George Regional Museum

Another outstanding feature of the plan was The Crescents at the western edge of the townsite. When the plans for the layout of the city's streets were revealed, property owners in Fort George claimed that the series of curved streets at the western edge of the townsite had been deliberately placed there to increase the distance between a station on First Avenue and the centre of Fort George.

In a letter written to the Board of Railway Commissioners in June 1915, one of the Fort George landowners, A.S. Norton of New York, said:

. . . it was a monstrous thing to do, to throw artificial obstacles in the way of the growth of the town in the one direction left open by nature. But this is precisely what these experts did do by creating the artificial barrier known as The Crescents to the west . . . Any man who knows anything about cities can see by a glance at the plan that a vicious angle was interposed to block traffic . . . going west . . .

An examination of the Index of the Municipal Roll for 1915 reveals Norton was not the only non-Canadian caught up in Hammond's plans. It contains the names of property owners who gave addresses from 12 countries: Canada, the United States, England, Scotland, Wales, Norway, Germany, Austria, Spain, New Zealand, Australia, and the Panama Canal zone.

THE BATTLE FOR INCORPORATION

Since 1911 the district had been administered by government agent Thomas Herne from his offices near the Hudson's Bay Company fort. Without the taxing powers of a municipality, the three communities—Prince George, Fort George, and South Fort George—found it difficult to provide their residents with needed electrical service, water supply, fire protection, schools, and hospitals. In August 1913 South Fort George became the first of the three communities to file an application for incorporation with the provincial government.

In the spring of the following year the residents of Fort George, led by Harry G. Perry, the president of the Fort George Board of Trade, protested South Fort George's application for incorporation. Confronted with a controversy, the government quickly withdrew, suggesting the neighboring townsites should meet and agree on a joint incorporation plan. A committee was established which quickly reached an agreement to include sections of the three townsites in an incorporation application. This application, covering 1,926.4 acres, was submitted in June 1914.

But the railway's lawyer, Hugh Hansard, objected, saying Prince George would be the centre of the development and it was unreasonable to expect its residents to bear the costs of providing services to those living in the two outlying communities. In July the railway company provided a special train to bring Premier William Bowser to Prince George to meet with the incorporation committee. At this meeting Hansard said that the railway, in return for supporting the committee's incorpo-

The east side of Central Avenue in Fort George was destroyed by fire in 1912. Courtesy, Provincial Archives of British Columbia

ration application, wanted an exemption from taxation until 1921 on all land used for railway purposes within the city boundaries.

But when the railway company made its formal offer in August, a new condition had been added requiring the station be built at the north end of George Street. In return the company had agreed to pay $14,000 in taxes before 1922 and $54,000 over the following 15 years, or an average of $3,600 per year.

While the railway was manoeuvring to get its station located at the north end of George Street, where it wanted it, the joint incorporation committee was trying to establish a boundary for the townsite. Hansard insisted the railway company wanted only the Prince George townsite included. His cause was aided when, on December 29, South Fort George withdrew from the incorporation committee. The residents of Fort George were determined to have the committee's recommendations go forward, even with the South Fort George land removed.

At a mass meeting held on January 12, 1915, in the newly constructed Princess Theatre on the southwest corner of Vancouver Street and Third Avenue, the committee failed to obtain support for its smaller incorporation plan. Instead, the meeting was disrupted by verbal attacks on the Fort George townsite representatives, led by three residents of Prince George: James Armstrong, agent for the Grand Trunk Pacific; real estate agent Fred Ruggles; and John Daniell, publisher of the *Prince George Post*. It was later claimed the three men had developed a plan to derail the committee's proposal during secret meetings with Hansard who, as the railway's lawyer, wanted only the Prince George townsite incorporated.

Whoever was responsible, the result was that on January 15, 1915, a separate incorporation plan for the 1,077 acres in the railway company's town plan was filed in Victoria by the Prince George Incorporation Committee. Three days later Fort George residents filed an incorporation

Government agent Thomas Herne, left, stands with the Grand Jury of the first assizes held in Prince George, on June 11, 1919. Courtesy, Provincial Archives of British Columbia

The first mayor of Prince George, W.G. Gillett, was elected on May 20, 1915. Courtesy, Fraser-Fort George Regional Museum

plan which included 1,361 acres from both townsites. Despite a recommendation by government engineer R.H. Thompson that the Fort George residents' application be accepted, the government announced on February 11, 1915, that it would incorporate land in the Prince George townsite. It is likely the number of voters in the two communities influenced the government's decision. By this time there were reported to be more than 2,000 people living in Prince George and 326 people living in Fort George.

The private members' bill incorporating the city was approved by the B.C. legislature on March 15, 1915. The bill was necessary because few people had resided in the area long enough to be legally able to vote or run for public office. Therefore the bill also enfranchised men who would otherwise have been unable to vote. (In 1915 Canadian women were not permitted to vote.)

The location of the station was also the main issue in the city's first municipal election on May 20, 1915. Building contractor William Gillett, a supporter of a station located at Maple Street, received 290 votes to become the first mayor. His opponent, real estate agent Neil Gething, a supporter of the railway company's plan to build the station on George Street, received 190 votes. Voters also approved Prince George over Fort George as the name for the new city by a vote of 153 to 13.

Since the new city had no money, Mayor Gillett signed a personal note to provide money for the operating budget until it was possible to assess and levy taxes. During his first term as mayor, Gillett used his personal loan as a weapon. During debates over the location of the station he would threaten to resign, knowing it would mean the bank would cancel the city's operating loan.

The newly incorporated city did not flourish. The railway construction boom died, men were enlisting in the services and leaving for overseas, and, as people turned their attention to World War I, the land boom in the central-interior died. Soon after the 1921 final ruling by the Board of Railway Commissioners, Hammond disappeared. Since the records of the Natural Resources Security Company were destroyed, no one knows whether Hammond left the area as a bankrupt or a rich man.

In 1953 Central Fort George finally became part of the City of Prince George. At that time the townsite Hammond had surveyed was used to provide homesites for people who came to the area from the prairies when the lumber industry began rapidly expanding.

On January 1, 1975, South Fort George became part of the city during an amalgamation of outlying areas. At that time the city boundaries were expanded to include developed properties along the Hart Highway, Highway 16 west, and Pineview.

WHAT'S IN A NAME?

There is a long-standing controversy over the Grand Trunk Pacific Railway's choice of the name Prince George for the community at the junction of the Fraser and Nechako rivers.

The company gave two reasons for its choice. In 1914 vice-president Morley Donaldson said it had been named after the ruling King George V. But, before he was crowned, King George was actually Prince Edward, so the explanation seems unlikely.

In an internal company note written in December 1911, Grand Trunk Pacific president Charles Hays put forth another reason for the choice of the name. He said the name Prince George had been chosen because it would ensure that the company's new townsite was ". . . permanently distinguished from the numerous towns now called Fort George, South Fort George, etc., which are in the vicinity" and also make it clear none of the other towns carried the company's endorsement.

When E.J. Chamberlin, who had succeeded Hays as president of the company, announced in 1913 that Prince George would be the official name of the new townsite, businessmen in Hammond's Fort George townsite launched an attack through the provincial government to have the new name set aside. They felt it threatened the future of their fledgling community by creating confusion about the true location of the townsite.

The businessmen forwarded a petition which read in part: "If there is one thing B.C. has stood for in the past it is that the works of those who have rough graded the paths of progress . . . shall not ruthlessly and unreasonably be torn from under them."

But it was all to no avail and the Prince George townsite was officially registered in Victoria.

In recent years a third explanation has arisen for the choice of Prince George as the name of the city. It holds that the city was named after Prince George, the youngest brother of King George VI and the uncle of Queen Elizabeth II.

Prince George, who later became the Duke of Kent, was the fourth of King George V's five children. He married the elegant Greek princess Marina in 1934. The couple had three children: Edward, Alexandra, and Michael.

Prince George was killed in an air crash in Scotland in August 1942 while serving as a wing commander in the Royal Air Force. His flight from Invergordon to Iceland aboard a Sunderland flying boat had run into a storm in northwestern Scotland, and the plane crashed into the side of a mountain.

*Saint George's Anglican Church
in Fort George was constructed
by the Reverend Isaac Williams.
Courtesy, Provincial Archives
of British Columbia*

IV

BODY, MIND, AND SOUL

Without educational advantages for the children surely no town can be considered to be worthy of its name and the fact that South Fort George now boasts of a school which is well-attended . . . gives this place a vastly added importance in the estimation of those families who are settling here.

With these words on September 5, 1910, the editor of the *Fort George Herald* saluted the opening of the first government school in what was to become Prince George. The school was located in South Fort George near the northwest intersection of what is now Queensway and Thapage Lane, in a building rented for $30 a month from the Northern Development Company.

The editorial reflects the importance the early settlers placed on the provision of schools, hospitals, and churches, for without them families were unlikely to remain in the community. It is no coincidence, therefore, that the arrival of the first white women in South Fort George in the spring of 1910 was followed by the openings of the first school that September and a hospital and churches within a year.

These institutions were signs that the area around Fort George was moving out of a century dominated by fur-trading, toward a future of permanent settlement.

The need for a public school in South Fort George was first raised at a meeting held in October 1909. By the conclusion of the meeting, the residents had established a school board composed of former freetrader and store owner Alexander G. Hamilton, Hudson's Bay Company factor James Cowie, and farmer James Bovyer. The newly elected board was authorized to begin advertising immediately for a teacher for the school.

Until a qualified teacher could be found, Mr. Cosgrove, a graduate of Princeton University, volunteered to fill the position. He and Miss L. Bradey taught until a qualified teacher, Mrs. A.B. Campbell, arrived several weeks after school had opened. By this time attendance was up to 24, with 9 white and 15 native students. In 1912 the students were moved into a new two-room school near what is now the west end of

On June 24, 1915, school-children gathered in The Island Cache, now known as Cottonwood Island Park, for this merry picnic with their parents. Courtesy, Provincial Archives of British Columbia

Hamilton Avenue.

Three miles to the west, George Hammond, the ebullient promoter of Fort George, was also aware of the importance of having a school on his town-site. In 1910 he had a log schoolhouse built for the five school-age children then living in the community and, since it was a private school, appointed Methodist minister Alfred Bell and his wife as Fort George's first teachers.

In the spring of 1911 Jennie Baker took over the teaching duties in Fort George, and in the fall of that year Miss M. Dodd was hired as the teacher. During the 1911-1912 school year the trustees of the Fort George school were Fred Shearer, W.R. Bookhout, and J.W. Scott. In 1913 William Bell became the teacher of the 24 students then enrolled at Fort George.

EDUCATION PROBLEMS

But all was not well in the schools of South Fort George and Fort George. In 1911 J.T. Pollock, inspector of schools for the district, criticized the school trustees for the lack of basic teaching materials and supplies for the students. At that time all freight was carried into the area over the Blackwater Road or by stern-wheeler. Therefore it required consider-able long-range planning to have all the school supplies for the coming year delivered when classes began in September.

Another problem was that although the teachers in both schools were poorly qualified when they arrived, once they had gained one or two years of teaching experience they were able to obtain employment in and move on to other more established communities in southern B.C. This meant the schools near Fort George were often staffed with poorly trained and inexperienced teachers.

Soon the residents of Fort George were complaining bitterly about the lack of provincial support for their school. In 1913 the acting chairman of the Fort George school board, Charles Moore (after whom Moore's Meadow is named) wrote a letter to the Minister of Education, saying the 75 students in the community were attending classes in a 23-by-28-foot building equipped with only eight desks, a few maps, and a blackboard, while students in South Fort George enjoyed classes in a large, provincially built school which was only half occupied.

The Fort George citizens' complaints were heard, and by August 2, 1913, the *Fort George Tribune* announced that contractor Donald Matheson had started construction on a new schoolhouse. This school was built at 2955 Third Avenue, where it can be seen today as part of the Fort George Central School.

When the residents of South Fort George and Fort George began moving into Prince George upon incorporation in 1915, the student population in the two outlying communities declined rapidly.

Prince George's first city council moved quickly to ensure its residents had schools to which they could send their children. The first school board—chairman Peter Wilson and trustees A.H. Mahan, Charles Leathley, and Hiram Carney—was elected on May 20, 1915, during the first civic elections.

One of the initial acts of the city's first aldermen was to prepare monetary by-laws to build schools and a city hall and to install water and electric systems in the new community.

Ratepayers approved the four monetary by-laws and in 1916 construction began on two schools: a four-room elementary school near Winnipeg Street and Seventh Avenue known as Baron Byng, and a secondary school near Queensway and 15th Avenue in the Millar Addition. The prin-

Baron Byng school, left, was built in 1916 to be used as an elementary school. Then, following the construction of King George V Elementary, right, in 1918, it became the district's secondary school, replacing the Millar Addition School. Courtesy, Provincial Archives of British Columbia

Millar Addition School, on the west side of Queensway, near 15th Avenue, was the first secondary school in the area. Courtesy, Provincial Archives of British Columbia

cipal, Miss W.L. Hammond, and three other teachers, Elizabeth Milligan, Charlotte Warner, and Mrs. G.E. Cook, were hired to teach the city's 180 students. Salaries averaged $100 per month, higher than the provincial average of $780 per year.

These new schools replaced the three small cottages at the corner of Fifth Avenue and Vancouver Street which, under the direction of Hammond, had served as the community's school since the fall of 1914.

But these were not the city's first schools. According to pioneer resident Jane Kennedy, daughter of Prince George's first school board chairman, Peter Wilson, the first school in the city was at the west end of Third Avenue. She described it as "an old red tin school" with two rooms separated by a partial partition.

Kennedy described what it was like to walk to school from their home in The Cache:

It was cold during the winter, awfully cold. We lived in the Cache and there were six of us trundling across the tracks and we'd all been warned not to crawl over the working places for the trains and we all did it because if you didn't you walked miles around the end. We were all scared to death of the cows that were down there. On winter days we used to carry a bucket of soup to eat when we were at school. We heated it on the stove at the old school because that was going to be our lunch.

Another pioneer resident who also attended classes in the three schools was Georgina Williams, the first non-native child born in the area. Williams said that one of the cottages had been built up on pilings because there was a deep pool of water under it. She remembered a tragic accident when a student, Sidney Oakley, drowned while playing in the pool when his rubber boots filled with water and pulled him under the surface.

Throughout this period the community was very involved with the schools. The June 15, 1915 edition of the *Fort George Herald* gave this Dickensian description of the year-end school picnic held at The Cache in June of that year:

In the afternoon pupils, teachers, parents and trustees gathered "at the island" for a picnic. Judging from the reports of the kiddies it was the biggest time in the country's history. There were games with races, all sorts of competitions with prizes attached, ice cream, oranges and the most gorgeous spread of eatables that ever preceded a colicky and troublous night. Not a fistic encounter was staged among the young hopefuls, while the girls of the school were as dainty and immaculate as dream angels. The grownups had just as much fun as the kids and chairman Wilson of the board of trustees was the busiest and happiest man in four counties.

Students sit with their hands behind their backs at the wooden desks of the newly opened King George V Elementary school. Courtesy, Fraser-Fort George Regional Museum

Another indication of the community's interest in the schools was the monthly publication of senior students' marks in the newspaper.

By 1916 the schools were again overcrowded and trustees were forced to rent classroom space outside the schools. The classroom shortage was alleviated in 1918 by the construction of a new eight-room elementary school which became known as King George V in 1921. Shortly after the new school was completed and the elementary school classes were relocated there, the high school classes were moved into Baron Byng school.

Throughout this period the area suffered from a chronic shortage of qualified teachers. In 1920 the condition became so bad in Prince George that the district school inspector gave the schools an "unfavorable standing."

The following year Julia Abbott was elected to the school board on her pledge to improve the operation of the school district. Abbott was the second woman to serve on the board. The first was Hannah Director, who was elected in 1918 and served as board chairperson during her first year.

In an interview in *The Citizen* printed on May 20, 1921, Abbott made charges that school trustees were not meeting regularly, minutes of the meetings that were held were unsatisfactory, accounting procedures were questionable, and teachers were being paid above the approved salary schedule. Since no copy of the schedule could be found, she said she intended to see to it that another salary schedule was adopted as soon as possible.

When the Depression hit, the city began looking for ways to reduce education costs. They first tried to enforce a previously approved regulation, levying a monthly charge of five dollars for each student attending high school whose parents or guardians did not reside in the city. But the provincial government ruled that the rural students were entitled to a free high school education. The school board then decided to save money by discontinuing business courses such as typing and bookkeeping.

When Department of Education minister George Weir visited the city in 1935, there was a heated public meeting during which residents complained about the unfairness of the education tax system. They complained that those whose taxes were so low they could afford to pay their entire bill were eligible to vote in the school elections, while those who paid more taxes were unable to vote because although they had paid more taxes than the voting group, they were unable to pay their entire tax bill. This was at the depth of the Depression when many people had been forced to accept government relief payments. Another complaint was heard about people being eligible to vote who had used their relief money to pay their taxes.

During the 10 years following 1930 the student population in Prince George dropped 29 percent, to 1,181, and the number of teachers dropped 27 percent, to 61. This resulted in more competition for teaching positions, forcing teachers to improve their qualifications if they wanted to keep their jobs. Teachers also tended to remain in the district longer because there were fewer jobs available in other parts of the province. The surplus of teachers ended when many of them joined the army after the outbreak of World War II.

In 1942 construction began on an army camp west of the city at which 6,000 to 8,000 men would be stationed. When the servicemen's families moved to be closer to their husbands and fathers, the student population again grew rapidly, and by 1944 the classroom shortage was once more a serious problem. Harry Perry, Minister of Education and former mayor of Prince George, visited the city to view the situation. Soon after his visit a contract was let for a new, $140,000 school at 1894 Ninth Avenue. The new school, named Prince George Junior-Senior High School, opened on January 2, 1945, and contained 10 classrooms, a gymnasium, and a library. It has been remodelled and now serves as the administration building for the school district.

In 1946 the school district was enlarged and given the name School District 57 as part of a provincial reorganization. In the fall of that year, under the direction of school board chairman Harold Moffat and high school principal Ray Williston, the school district moved three army barracks onto lots at the corner of Wainwright Street and Seventh

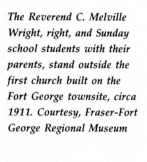

The Reverend C. Melville Wright, right, and Sunday school students with their parents, stand outside the first church built on the Fort George townsite, circa 1911. Courtesy, Fraser-Fort George Regional Museum

Avenue and renovated them into a dormitory for high school students from the small sawmill towns springing up amidst the nearby forests. The dormitory was opened in 1947 and served as a home away from home for rural students until 1977.

The district's problems did not end with World War II. At the conclusion of the war, the demand for lumber stimulated a boom in the local sawmill industry and trustees were called upon to provide elementary schools in many outlying areas. Portable schools were used as classrooms in the region's hundreds of small sawmills, and permanent schools were built in larger logging centres.

In the early 1950s School District 57 launched an aggressive drive to recruit better-qualified teachers. This was so successful it resulted in half the district's teachers having been trained outside of B.C. Unfortunately, many of these teachers did not find conditions in the district to their liking and, by 1955-1956, staff turnover had soared to 80 percent.

In 1962 the forerunner of the College of New Caledonia, the B.C. Vocational School, was constructed on the west side of the Bypass Highway by the provincial government at a cost of $1.7 million. When the building was opened in September, students were enrolled in six courses: heavy duty mechanics, auto mechanics, millwrighting, welding, commercial subjects, and practical nursing.

The Catholic church had been developing its own schools. Sacred Heart Elementary School on Patricia Boulevard was opened in 1949. Bishop Fergus O'Grady led the campaign to open Prince George College in College Heights in 1956. It provided secondary-school instruction to the children of Catholic parents, many of whom had emigrated from Europe. In addition, the college served as a residential high school for Indian students from throughout central and northern B.C.

Throughout the period from 1910 to 1960, Indian children from the nearby Shelley Reserve rarely attended the public elementary schools. When they reached the age of six years the majority of them left home to attend the Catholic residential school at Lejacq, west of Vanderhoof.

All the Catholic schools in the area were operated by the Order of the Oblates of Mary Immaculate, who began their missionary work in New Caledonia with the arrival of Father Demers in September 1842. The Catholic school system in Prince George was expanded in 1960 by the addition of St. Mary's School on Gillett Street.

MEETING MEDICAL NEEDS

In addition to spiritual and educational work, another Oblate, Father Nicolas Coccola, who arrived in New Caledonia in 1905, also provided rudimentary medical services before a Western-educated doctor arrived in the area.

Since Father Coccola's headquarters were in Fort St. James and he only visited Prince George once a year, during most of the year the pioneers living near Fort George relied on home remedies, the Hudson's Bay factor, and Indian medicines to treat their illnesses. There is a report that a man who had his feet severely burned aboard a stern-wheeler was cured by an Indian healer.

As the population grew, there were many more stories of the hardships suffered by the pioneers at Fort George, who lived 100 miles from the hospital at Quesnel. A 1908 edition of the *Fort George Herald* tells of

Father Coccola, and the teaching nuns of the Order of Mary Immaculate, posed on the steps of the residential school at Lejacq for this photograph. The Indian girls are seen wearing the uniform prescribed by the Catholic Church. Courtesy, Fraser-Fort George Regional Museum

Above: These Indian boys were among many taken from their homes and placed in the Catholic church's residential school at Lejacq. There they were forbidden to speak their own language, and subjected to rigorous religious and educational training. Father Coccola, one of the priests responsible for the school, stands in the background. Courtesy, Fraser-Fort George Regional Museum

Right: Dr. Eddie Lyon, centre, was the first president of the Prince George Branch of the Canadian Medical Association. He stands outside the city's first hospital, built near the intersection of 13th Avenue and Lethbridge Street. Courtesy, Fraser-Fort George Regional Museum

the case of "Surveyor O.B.N. Wilkie who now lies in most critical condition in Kamloops Hospital with an abscess of the throat brought on by a case of tonsilitis," and the case of "Engineer Daly of the steamer *Chilco*, who was obliged to leave here on the last boat for Quesnel to obtain medical attention for a case of blood poisoning."

In March 1910 John Houston, publisher of the area's first newspaper, died of pneumonia while friends were pulling him to Quesnel over the Blackwater Trail on a toboggan.

A small log hospital was built in South Fort George in 1911. It was used by the area's first Western-educated doctor, Dr. L.B. Lazier, and registered nurse, Miss B.A. Fry.

It was replaced later that year by a two-storey frame building on the west side of Central Street between Fifth and Third avenues. By that time Dr. Hugh McSorley, Dr. W. Cecil Swenerton, and later that year, Dr. Carl Ewert had arrived to provide medical care to the community.

A Hospital Auxiliary was formed in 1910 with Mrs. James Cowie, the wife of the Hudson's Bay factor, as its first president. The auxiliary raised funds by holding teas and hot dog sales and providing catering services for local events. The money was used to purchase drapes, bed linens, and other supplies for the private nursing hospitals being opened in the three adjacent townsites. In August 1913 a nurse identified only as Miss Kellett announced she was prepared to provide nursing care for private patients either in her own home on Central Avenue or at the home of the patient. In Prince George Miss F.M. Maundrell operated a private nursing hospital in the building which now stands at 1584 Eighth Avenue. A three-bed private hospital was also reported to have been opened in South Fort George.

In 1912 another hospital was built by the railway construction company of Foley, Welch and Stewart on the south bank of the Nechako River in the area now occupied by Cottonwood Island Park. Dr. W.A. Richardson, who had been hired to provide medical care for the railway employees, also attended to the medical needs of the residents of the nearby communities.

The inadequacy of the hospitals in the area became apparent during

The Pine Manor Hospital, which stood near the site of the present-day Simon Fraser Hospital, served the city until the end of World War II. At that time the city acquired an 80-bed military hospital, built to serve the Canadian soldiers stationed in the city during the war. Courtesy, Fraser-Fort George Regional Museum

the flu epidemic of 1918 when schools and hotels were turned into emergency hospitals. This resulted in a call for a larger hospital for Prince George, and a Hospital Society was incorporated later that year. In May 1919 the society had a 30-bed hospital built near the present-day site of Simon Fraser Hospital. It was called Pine Manor.

Pioneer resident Alice Clark recalled how auxiliary members sewed and repaired bedding, gowns, diapers, and layettes for the new publicly owned hospital. They also collected donations and held raffles, dinners, and dances to raise money to purchase equipment such as X-ray machines for the new hospital:

We put in hours. I remember standing at the bottom of Connaught [Hill], standing there, [snow] half-way to your knees, trying to get the hot dogs and coffee and what have you to the people at the ski jump. We used to take a team of horses and go and gather stuff around—potatoes from one place, someone else would give us some carrots and supplies for the hospital. That's the way we did it at first.

By 1923, despite the efforts of the volunteers, the hospital was experiencing financial problems and the Catholic church was approached to take over its operation. However, no nursing sisters would agree to assume responsibility for operating the hospital and the financial problems continued until 1939, when the hospital society inaugurated a community-based health insurance plan in which families paying $1.25 per month received free hospital services.

The doctors were also becoming more organized and, at a conference of central-interior B.C. doctors held in Prince George during July 1929, they decided to establish a local branch of the Canadian Medical Association. Dr. Edward "Eddie" Lyon was elected the first president. Serving on the executive board with him were vice-president Dr. Gerald Rumsey Baker of Quesnel, secretary-treasurer Dr. Carl Ewert, and directors Dr. J.T. Steele of Giscome and Dr. Harold Trefry of Prince George.

At the end of World War II the city acquired the 80-bed military hospital built to serve the soldiers stationed in Prince George during the war. Its capacity was gradually expanded to 110 beds. The sprawling military hospital had a series of 120-foot-long wards designed to prevent the destruction of the whole hospital by one bomb. This design led one

By the spring of 1959, work-men were placing the finishing touches on the 125-bed hospital built to replace the former army hospital that had served the city since the end of World War II. Courtesy, Fraser-Fort George Regional Museum

patient to suggest that the nurses working in the 24-patient wards should have been paid by the mile for working there. But nurses claimed the big wards made it easier for a small staff to care for many patients because they were in the self-contained wards which permitted the nurses to observe all their patients from the nursing station.

In 1955 the hospital's taxing authority was expanded into the surrounding districts when the letters patent was issued establishing the Prince George Hospital Improvement District.

In May 1958 the sod was turned for a new 125-bed hospital at 2000 15th Avenue. Due to a series of expansions, this hospital can now accommodate 449 patients, including 72 extended care patients, 44 babies, and 37 chemical dependency patients.

When the hospital was officially opened on January 16, 1960, the first patient through the doors was 108-year-old Grannie Seymour, daughter of James Bouchey (an employee of the Hudson's Bay Company trading post at Fort St. James) and a princess of the Fort Simpson band.

SERVING SPIRITUAL NEEDS

Seymour had been a young woman in the late 1870s when one of the area's first permanent missionaries, Father J.M. Lejacq, supervised the construction of Prince George's first church on the Indian reserve lands now occupied by Fort George Park. In August 1885, Father Lejacq was replaced by Father Adrien Gabriel Morice. Throughout his 19 years in New Caledonia Morice travelled extensively, gathering information on the Carrier language and Dene history, anthropology, and ethnography.

Father Nicolas Coccola was assigned to replace Father Morice in 1905. In his memoirs he describes a scene at the church on the Indian Reserve near Fort George:

In Fort George the Indians had a beautiful church built by themselves and kept very neat and tidy; so much so that white people, when the construction of the Grand Trunk Pacific Railway began to be talked about, and the townsite was located at South Fort George, the people would find their great pleasure in coming to the Indian church and the Indians, out of politeness, moved away and from the windows and doors of the building take part in the services and allow the white visitors to sit in.

Services continued to be held at the Catholic church on the reserve until 1913, when the Indians sold their land to the Grand Trunk Pacific and moved to their present reserve at Shelley.

When the white population increased, mass was also celebrated in the Birch's Hall in South Fort George until August 12, 1914, when a new Catholic church in the Millar Addition was officially blessed by Father Louis Rivet. This church served the Catholic congregation until the Sacred Heart Church was blessed on Christmas Eve 1924. A new, larger Catholic church was opened on the same site on April 5, 1961.

The first permanent Protestant missionary, the Reverend Alfred Bell of the Methodist church, arrived in South Fort George on June 24, 1910.

Left: The first Catholic church was officially blessed by Father L. Rivet, O.M.I., in August 1914. Courtesy, Provincial Archives of British Columbia

Two days later he held his first church service in a 40-foot-long tent he had set up on the southeast corner of Hamilton Avenue and Queensway. South Fort George must not have been fertile ground for the young Methodist minister, for he was not successful in establishing a permanent church there.

His lack of success was probably due to the wide-open, high-flying lifestyle of many residents. Because South Fort George was located near the sternwheeler landing, it quickly developed into a whoop-it-up, frontier-style town. Construction workers, speculators, businessmen, and settlers swarmed into the area after it was announced that a major terminal of the railway would be built near the junction of the Fraser and Nechako rivers. The 120-foot-long bar at the Hotel Northern was a major attraction. It is said people lined up six deep in front of that bar, with drinks being passed to someone at the back of the line often consumed by another thirsty customer before they got to the person who had paid for them. Business was also reported to be good in another section of South Fort George where four bawdy-houses had been built by a woman whom the newspapers of the day euphemistically referred to as "businesswoman Irene Jordan."

The Reverend Bell and the Reverend C. Melville Wright, a Presbyterian missionary, found more fertile ground in Fort George, and when Irene Jordan attempted to expand her business there, the indignant church members launched a successful protest. Although Jordan had already purchased property and started construction of a house, she was forced to abandon her plans. For the time being, Fort George could point to South Fort George as the home of "fallen women" and the evils of strong drink.

In June 1913 the Reverend Wright created a stir in the area when he was quoted in the *Toronto Globe* as telling a large missionary meeting in Toronto he had ". . . walked 300 miles from the very gates of hell" to attend the meeting. When he was asked to describe the vices which were rampant in the community he said, "In the first place the liquor traffic is flourishing. There are two

This Methodist church once stood on Third Avenue across from the Provincial Government Building. It was opened May 9, 1915, by the Reverend H. Lloyd Morrison and is believed to be the first church built in Prince George following the city's incorporation. Courtesy, Fraser-Fort George Regional Museum

saloons with four to six bartenders each. The bankers have told me their deposits have dwindled with the granting of the [liquor] licenses. Then there is the segregated district, four big houses with 30 women in South Fort George two blocks from Knox Church."

It is reported that the residents of South Fort George gave Wright a cool reception on his return. But he was able to convince them he'd been misquoted by explaining that when a former missionary in the area, the Reverend R.P. MacKay, introduced him at the meeting, MacKay had said that in order to get to the meeting Wright had travelled 300 miles to reach a railway. Then, after describing how Wright was succeeding in spite of many obstacles, MacKay had went on to say, "But the work is now so firmly established that the gates of hell shall not prevail against it."

With Hammond's backing the Presbyterian church flourished. In 1913 Wright obtained a $5,000 loan from a Vancouver bank to construct an

In 1911, St. Stephen's Church was built by the Anglican order on the bank of the Fraser River, in South Fort George. Courtesy, Provincial Archives of British Columbia

Following its move from Fort George to the corner of 15th Avenue and Ingledew Street, the St. Michael and All Angels' Church was subject to charges of "theft." Courtesy, Provincial Archives of British Columbia

impressive housing for the First Presbyterian Church in Fort George, dedicated on June 28, 1914.

By the end of 1914 there were seven active churches in the area: Sacred Heart Catholic Church; three Protestant churches (Knox in South Fort George, St. Andrew's in Prince George, and First Presbyterian in Fort George); two Anglican churches (St. Stephen's in South Fort George and St. George's in Fort George); and First Methodist Church in Prince George.

By 1916 Lutheran missionaries were holding occasional services in the area, and by 1925 they had acquired the former Knox Church building on Patricia Boulevard and renamed it Connaught Hill Lutheran Church.

In September 1923 the Cariboo Presbytery of the United Church of Canada opened a school home at 1268 Fifth Avenue for girls who wished to attend school in Prince George. Although the school was intended to accommodate high school students, in 1924 it began accepting younger students and some boys. The home continued to operate until it was forced to close in 1929, when the number of students living there had dwindled to six.

Knox Church, at the corner of Brunswick Street and Fifth Avenue, was officially opened on November 5, 1922. Earlier that year the remaining Presbyterian members in Fort George transferred their membership to Knox Church and on June 10, 1925, as part of the national terms of union signed by the two church bodies, the Methodist and Presbyterian churches in the area were united into what is now known as the United Church of Canada.

In 1911 an Anglican priest, the Reverend Isaac Williams, was stationed at Fort George, which was then the most northerly posting in the mission district of the Diocese of New Westminster. With the help of volunteers, he had a small church dedicated to St. George built in Fort George in 10 days. Later that same year, a second, larger church dedicated to St. Stephen was built in South Fort George.

Williams continued his work in the two communities until 1913, when he was succeeded by the Reverend Ralph Sadler. Serving as an assistant lay reader to Sadler in South Fort George was Samuel Pollinger. He returned to Prince George following his ordination and continued to serve throughout the area until he was elected a bishop of the church in 1941.

The Anglican congregation's search for a permanent home in Prince George led to what came to be known as "the Stolen Church." For a period during 1914, the Anglican, Presbyterian, and Methodist congregations all held church services in a store on Third Avenue and, during the summer of that year, Anglican church services were held in one of the three school buildings near the corner of Vancouver Street and Fifth Avenue. When school resumed they rented Andersen's Hall at 1362 Seventh Avenue.

By 1919 the Anglican congregation had acquired lots on the southeast corner of Ingledew Street and 15th Avenue and moved St. George's Church there from Fort George, renaming it St. Michael and All Angels'. But members of the Fort George congregation charged that some of the legal niceties had not been completed before the church was moved to its new location. Therefore, they said, the church had been stolen.

Bishop Adam of New Westminster and Cariboo clarified the matter when he wrote to the church members in Fort George and Prince George on May 21, 1919, saying he had requested the church be moved on the basis of a recommendation from an archdeacon in 1916. He said that when he had visited the church the year before there were "no wardens nor any church committee . . . and as the church was falling into decay, no service being held in it for two years, I decided to take action."

The church remained at that site until 1951, when the congregation built a hall at 1505 Fifth Avenue which it used until a building was completed beside the hall and dedicated by the Right Reverend Ralph Dean, Fifth Bishop of Cariboo, on October 22, 1963.

As the city's population grew and prospered so did its churches, and by 1987 there were 44 churches active in Prince George, including four Catholic, six Baptist, four United, two Anglican, two Lutheran, and one Presbyterian.

This interior view of St. Michael and All Angels' Church, at the corner of 15th Avenue and Ingledew Street, was photographed circa 1925. Courtesy, Fraser-Fort George Regional Museum

Posing for this photo in June 1943, the members of the Knox United Church session are; back row, left to right, R.G. Newton, Dave Fraser, the Reverend Francis Edwin Runnalls, A. Hunter, H. Hill, and, front row, left to right, Ken Irwin, John Mallis, John Gaul, and H.J. Hocking. Courtesy, Provincial Archives of British Columbia

The Hotel Northern in South Fort George, was reputed to have the longest bar west of Chicago. The hotel was the setting for many pranks and stories of "early days" in the three Georges. Courtesy, Provincial Archives of British Columbia

V

A COMMUNITY AT PLAY

Hotels—especially the rowdy Hotel Northern in South Fort George—played a large part in the social life in the three Georges during the first two decades of this century.

Tales told about the volume of alcohol that flowed across the Hotel Northern's long mahogany bar may differ, but there is no doubt that the hotel was very busy when railway construction workers, pre-emptors, settlers, speculators, and the just plain curious began streaming into South Fort George to have a look at the community being promoted as "the Chicago of the North."

The traffic in front of the bar was reported to have been so heavy that the pinewood plank floor was repeatedly worn out by the men's heavy work boots. Bouncers hauled those who had passed out into a "Snake Room" behind the bar where they could sleep off the effects of alcohol undisturbed. Depending on the storyteller, either 12, 14, 18, or 24 bartenders were necessary to keep the thirsty men supplied with their favorite brand of poison.

The original Hotel Northern was built in 1910 at the corner of Rose Avenue and Fourth Street in South Fort George by Albert "Al" Johnson and Robert Michael Burns. By December of that year it became the first hotel in the area with a license to serve alcohol. Both men had previously operated hotels in other boom towns in the interior—Johnson at Quesnel and Burns at Port Essington on the Skeena River—so they were well aware of the value of a liquor license in a pioneer community.

The Hotel Northern burned to the ground on July 1, 1911—a not uncommon event during a time when buildings were heated by wood-burning stoves. After the fire Johnson and Burns agreed to dissolve their partnership, and Johnson rebuilt the Hotel Northern at the corner of Hamilton Avenue and Third Street. It was this hotel that earned a reputation for its busy bar.

Pranks and practical jokes were a common feature of life in the pioneer community, and Johnson was the perpetrator of one prank which cost him a free round of drinks.

According to pioneer resident Ted Williams, Johnson sponsored an

63

event during the 1911 Dominion Day celebrations in South Fort George in which a purse with the corner of a $20 bill showing from its top was nailed to the top of a tall greased pole. The man who could somehow slither up the greasy pole and retrieve the purse would win the $20. After a mad scramble, one man finally reached the top, grabbed the purse, and returned to the ground where, upon opening the purse, he found the only thing it contained was the corner of the $20 bill which could be seen from the ground. The mob of men, many of whom had already been celebrating in Johnson's bar, marched to the hotel demanding the money. Johnson was reported to have hidden until the mob was pacified with an offer of free drinks.

Prominent citizens of South Fort George, and local area residents, posed for this photograph on June 12, 1911, during the farewell banquet for James Cowie, manager of the Hudson's Bay Company. Courtesy, Fraser-Fort George Regional Museum

VICES ABOUND

Gambling was also a common activity among the railway construction workers. In 1913 the *Fort George Herald* reported that provincial police chief Dunwoody and constables Aldrich, Ealch, and Nunnelly arrested seven men during a raid on a gambling operation carried on in a tent in what is now Cottonwood Island Park. According to the newspaper report the police confiscated $116 and a quantity of gambling paraphernalia after finding ". . . the dive was running full blast in the tent north of the Grand Trunk Pacific track, when the police arrived on the scene and interrupted the 'lil game uv draw.'"

During their trial it was shown that the operators of the gambling tent and some of the gamblers were known crooks who had been using small hand mirrors to determine the denominations of other players' cards. According to the report of the trial: "One of these tin horns tried to explain away the suspicions created by the crooked appliance by saying he used it to look at his teeth. Magistrate Herne failed to bite however."

The provincial police were responsible for policing duties in the area until a city police force was formed when the City of Prince George was incorporated in 1915. A board of commissioners headed by the mayor was responsible for controlling the city's police until June 15, 1925, when policing duties were again assumed by the B.C. provincial police. The Royal Canadian Mounted Police took over from the provincial police on August 15, 1950.

In his book *The New Garden of Canada*, F.A. Talbot used these words to describe the activity at a poolroom of the day:

When the frequenters grew tired of cue and ivories the tables were pushed into a corner and vents was found for exuberance in dancing to the strains of a wheezy, expiring gramophone, in footwear which could scarcely be described as ballroom, for heavy hobnailed half-inch soles clattered over the uneven knotty boards.

Since the majority of the city's first settlers were men, it was not surprising that a red-light district quickly sprang up in South Fort George. Pioneer resident Ted Williams recalls how, at the urging of the recently arrived ministry, a group called The Crusaders was established

in South Fort George in about 1911 with the aim of ridding the community of prostitution. Russell Peden chaired a meeting called to discuss the matter. But when a motion was passed calling for the removal of the ladies, Peden immediately turned the chair over to someone else and moved that another boatload of ladies be brought in.

Stampedes and horse races were features of the July l celebrations during the pioneer era in the three Georges. One of the first stampedes of which there is any record took place in South Fort George on July 1, 1908. Nineteen events were advertised and the prizes totalled $1,500. H. Smith was reported to have won the half-mile pony race from the Hotel Northern to Hamilton Avenue, both cowboy races were won by J. Bird's pony, the team of Paulittle and Dewiss won the two-mile canoe race, Maurice Quaw won the standing broad jump, and A. Leinke won the two-mile race. There were also prizes for the best waltzers and "grinning through a horse collar," in which a prize was given to the person who, using a horse collar to frame their face, could make the funniest expression.

In 1926, crowd surrounds the corral as riders prepare for a stampede at the fairgrounds then located near the junction of highways 16 and 97. Courtesy, Provincial Archives of British Columbia

SOCIAL ACTIVITIES

Less has been said about gentler social activities in the three Georges in which women, children, and families were involved. An examination of the newspapers of the day shows that dances, masquerades, concerts, and talent shows were common. One of the first dances of record was written up in the November 13, 1909, edition of the *Fort George Tribune*, which reported:

The first social function of the winter took place on Saturday night when the Comus Club gave a dance in honor of the 16th birthday of its genial president, George Forbes. Dancing was kept up until midnight. The Ladies attending being adherents of the church declined to dance on Sunday even to dance the Hudson Bay quadrille to music furnished by three of the best fiddlers in the whole of the Cariboo.

In November 1910 the captain, officers, and crew of the *BX* were the hosts of an informal dance on the lower deck of the stern-wheeler. The music for the occasion was provided by organist Charles Mills, violinist T. Sallis, mandolinist Harry Stoddard, and piccolo player Dave Anderson.

Other musicians whose names appear in the early reports of dances are violinists Ralph Johnston and R.T. Kerr, and harpists Mr. Tortorelli of Fort George and Jack Senior of South Fort George, who was known as a one-man band because he could play the mouth organ, drum, and harp all at one time.

After the incorporation of the City of Prince George, John Harmon "J.H." Johnson built a hotel, the Alexandra, on the southwest corner of Third Avenue and Brunswick Street in Prince George. The hotel was the scene of many formal social activities including afternoon tea dances, coming-out parties, and black-tie dances and receptions. Johnson had previously been the owner of the Fort George Hotel on the Fort George townsite which was destroyed by fire in 1914.

A ROYAL VISIT

The Alexandra was the scene of a particularly splendid party when the Duke and Duchess of Devonshire visited the city in 1919. Although this was during the prohibition, Johnson wanted to treat the duke to his favorite drink, a mint julep. According to a report carried in the *Fort George Tribune,* Johnson called on the police chief for help. He rounded up all the local bootleggers and ordered them to produce a case of whiskey or be charged with bootlegging the next day.

The whiskey was produced, Johnson served the duke several rounds of juleps, and an impromptu horse race was staged, since the duke was the owner of more than one champion racehorse. Several farm horses were gathered together for the event and the duke, dressed in a grey top hat and cutaway coat, watched the race down Third Avenue from the front of the Alexandra Hotel.

But the horses were not impressed by the royal spectator and, instead of racing straight down Third Avenue, galloped off in different directions. When he was asked what he thought of the horse race, the duke replied tactfully that he had never seen anything quite like it before.

As he left he was reported to have asked his aide, Harold MacMillan, who later became prime minister of Great Britain, to get a copy of the recipe for the mint juleps.

Pioneer resident Nellie Law, who was a waitress at the Alexandra Hotel at the time of the visit of the Duke and Duchess of Devonshire, said there was also an afternoon tea for the ladies and a big dinner in the evening. Legend has it that after the main course, she leaned over the duke's shoulder and said, "Hang on to your fork Duke, the pie is coming."

In a story which appeared in *The Province* on September 9, 1944, Christine Taylor reported her description of how Prince George residents made their way to formal dances:

We went to dances in backless dresses in 50 below zero, and we had to walk. The

men would not risk freezing their cars in such weather, but we bundled up in fur coats, three pair of heavy stockings, woollen hoods, and stopped at each house we passed, to thaw out our breath. Usually the thawing-out process was performed with the help of a good hot toddy.

Taylor wrote of another occasion when, as decoration for a dance, the railway company installed a replica of an entire engine across one side of the ballroom located on the second storey of a popular dance hall, the Ritts-Kifer, which had been constructed on George Street between Fourth and Fifth avenues in 1914.

LEISURE ACTIVITIES

Picnics were another pleasant pastime enjoyed by pioneer residents. An announcement in the July 25, 1914, edition of the *Fort George Tribune* extended an invitation from the officers and members of the Cariboo Women's Club to "the wives, mothers, maids together with the bachelors and benedicts of the district to join with them in a jolly picnic to be held on the Nechako Riverfront west of the mill in the afternoon of June 30. Come and try our Cariboo Chowder."

Rev. Francis Edwin Runnalls' book tells of a picnic cruise to Fort George Canyon which took place on July 1, 1918. The stern-wheeler left from Fort George and passed under the lifted centre span of the railway bridge and down the river to the picnic site at the north end of the canyon. There the passengers spent the day enjoying a sports program

Mrs. Somerton, Cowie, Beasley, Dixon, Taylor, Herne, and Hornsby, gathered for afternoon tea at the home of Mr. and Mrs. James Cowie, in what is now Fort George Park. Cowie was the manager of the Hudson's Bay Company Trading Post in Prince George until the post was closed in 1915. Courtesy, Provincial Archives of British Columbia

Above: In 1925, Harry Perry, standing at left, prepares to crown the second May Queen, Maude Renwick, near the Perrys' home, at the west end of 10th Avenue. Courtesy, Provincial Archives of British Columbia

A large brass band leads a parade on July 1, along George Street toward City Hall, circa 1920. In the background the tower of the fire hall is visible north of the Prince George Hotel. Courtesy, Provincial Archives of British Columbia

and a picnic supper before reboarding the stern-wheeler.

On August 26, 1921, a group called Canadian Chautauqua came to Prince George to present a series of performances by musicians, lecturers, and magicians in the Rex Theatre on George Street. Two theatres had been built on George Street by this time: the Rex and the Dreamland.

According to the August 12, 1921, edition of the *Prince George Leader,* the aim of Chautauqua was "to go to towns where it is needed most and bring before the minds of the people in a clear, forceful and fearless manner the questions that vex us today and as far as possible to find an answer to them."

Twelve different acts were offered during this first visit of Chautauqua, including Captain Dancey, an author, lecturer, and soldier; four female musicians, who called themselves the "Old Fashioned Girls"; Horace Smithey, a baritone; Arthur W. Evans, a Welsh lecturer; a trio of musicians from New York and Chicago; soprano Hazel B. Strayer; a magician and occultist named De Jen; and lecturer Captain Norman A. Imrie.

For 12 years beginning in 1953, the Alaska Music Trail began bringing four concerts a year to Prince George under the sponsorship of the Prince George Concert Association. Among the young artists who appeared in Prince George on this tour before going on to achieve international fame were baritone Louis Quilico, who appeared in Prince George in May 1958, and soprano Marilyn Horne, who entertained Prince George residents in December 1959. The concert association also sponsored the Prince George appearances of the Canadian Opera Company, the Hart House Orchestra, and the Vancouver Symphony.

Recreation was a vital part of pioneer life in Prince George. Intertown rivalries were established between hockey and baseball teams, and boxing matches were regularly staged in all three communities. The *Fort George Tribune* of June 20, 1914, reported Chet McIntyre was working hard to finish the Ritts-Kifer Hall in time for a boxing contest to be held there on Dominion Day. The interior of the hall was to be finished in wood, with a waxed floor for dancing and moveable bleachers for use at boxing shows and other contests. McIntyre, who was a light heavyweight, Eddie Franks, and Billy Soules were among the boxers who took part in the 1914 Dominion Day matches. Another well-known pioneer boxer was Billy Munro.

WINTER SPORTS
Winter skating parties were held on the Nechako River near the boat landing below the Fort George townsite,

Above: The ice on the Fraser River, near South Fort George, was smooth and thick when these skaters decided to have a skating party. Music was provided by harpist Jack Senior. Courtesy, Fraser-Fort George Regional Museum

Right: A crowd of construction workers gathered to watch this hockey game between railway workers and residents of the three Georges, in the Island Cache now known as Cottonwood Island Park. Courtesy, Provincial Archives of British Columbia

and on the numerous backwaters and sloughs around Prince George and South Fort George. These sloughs were all that remained of the beds that once carried the rivers over the townsite of Prince George. According to pioneer residents, a series of these interconnected sloughs once ran along the base of the bank on the north side of Patricia Boulevard, past City Hall, and into the slough which once covered the area west of Connaught Hill. Another series of interconnected sloughs ran from the Hudson's Bay slough around the north end of Peden Hill and onto land now occupied by Woodward's. Assman's slough, between First Avenue and the bank behind the Provincial Government Building on Third Avenue, was another spot where people would skate when the ice was safe. A bonfire would provide heat and light for night skating.

The first indoor ice-skating arena constructed on the Fort George townsite was flooded by bringing water up from the river in barrels. Within a few years of its completion, it collapsed under the weight of snow and was never replaced.

Following the incorporation of Prince George in 1915, an outdoor arena was constructed on the northwest corner of Fifth Avenue and Brunswick Street. In a tape recorded interview, pioneer resident Arthur Fisk said music for skating was provided by a gramophone. He recalled going outdoors one night when it was 40 degrees below zero, and being amused to hear the gramophone incongruously blaring the song "In the Good Old Summer Time" over the frigid city.

Harry Thacker flooded and maintained this outdoor rink and supervised the activities of several generations of residents who learned to skate on it and the covered natural ice arena that was opened in 1940 on the northeast corner of Seventh Avenue and Quebec Street.

But on February 6, 1956, the covered arena also collapsed. A sudden shift of the weight on the roof when a snow pack fell off one side was

Above: The members of the Prince George hockey team posed for this photo, at the outdoor arena, on the corner of Fifth Avenue and Brunswick Street, circa 1920. Courtesy, Olive Dodd

Left: Prince George had its own Canucks when this photograph was taken, circa 1920. Coach Joe Strobike stands to the left of the back row. Courtesy, Fraser-Fort George Regional Museum

blamed for the destruction. Fortunately, no one was in the building at the time.

The following year construction was begun on The Coliseum, the city's first artificial ice arena. The arena was opened in 1958. But in February 1969 an engineer declared the roof of the building unsafe, and it was closed while steel girders were installed over the roof for support. It was reopened the following year.

The sport of ski jumping flourished in Prince George during the early part of this century but has since disappeared. According to the February 1, 1931, edition of *The Province,* a Vancouver newspaper, Prince George enjoyed the distinction of having the only illuminated ski jump hill on the North American continent, and the second in the world. Kongsberg, Norway, was the first to introduce ski jumping at night. *The Province* reported that Prince George's ski jump, which was located on the northwest face of Connaught Hill, was constructed to Olympic standards and was similar to the one built at Lake Placid for the 1932 Olympics.

Among the skiers expected to come to Prince George that year for the western championships were N. Kaldahl of the Hollyburn Pacific Ski Club; Nip Stone, Lindsay Loutet, and W. Walkinshaw of the Grouse Mountain Ski Club; Frank Jacobson, Eric Sandstrom, and R.J. Verne of the Viking Club; and N. Jorstad of Winnipeg's Norge Ski Club. Peter Sandres was captain of the Prince George Club.

Curling emerged as another favorite wintertime

Above: This ski jump was built during the 1930s on the northwest face of Connaught Hill. Courtesy, Fraser-Fort George Regional Museum

Right: This curling rink on the west side of Connaught Hill, was the scene of many bonspiels between the years 1900 and 1930. Courtesy, Fraser-Fort George Regional Museum

activity. The first curling rink was located near the west end of Third Avenue. For many years the curlers gathered at a rink located near the northwest end of Connaught Hill, and following World War II a curling rink was constructed in the basement of the Civic Centre. All these rinks relied on natural ice, which meant some bonspiels were struggles to see who could slide the stones to the other end of the rink through the layer of water covering the ice. The city's first curling rink with artificially made ice was opened on the southwest corner of the junction of highways 16 and 97 in early 1956.

One of the city's most famous curling trophies is the Kelly Cup, presented to the club in 1927 by John Kelly, a jeweller and sports fan. The Kelly Cup Bonspiel, which has been held every year since 1927 except in 1943, when it was cancelled because of the war, was an important wintertime event in Prince George during the first half of this century. When employees entered the "spiel" they assumed their bosses would give them time off to play their games during working hours.

Another long-standing event in Prince George is the Prince George Fall Fair, now known as the Exhibition. The first fair was staged outdoors on the Fort George townsite on September 17 and 18, 1912. Later it was moved to the curling rink beside Connaught Hill, then to the arena on Quebec Street which eventually collapsed.

During the 1920s the fall fairs included sideshow attractions and concession stands, and had become such major events the two-day fairs were declared a civic holiday.

During the 1949 bonspiel, teams gathered on the ice for this photograph. The curling rink was located in the basement of the Civic Centre on Seventh Avenue. Courtesy, Fraser-Fort George Regional Museum

*Aliens living in the vicinity of
Prince George were rounded-up
and placed in this camp, near the
city following the outbreak of
World War I. Courtesy, Provincial
Archives of British Columbia*

VI
HARD TIMES

By the time Prince George was incorporated in 1915, the frenzy of real estate speculation in the city was already on the wane.

The main impetus for the real estate boom had been the construction of the Grand Trunk Pacific Railway. When the Canadian government entered World War I in August 1914, it put an end to any hope for further railway construction in the area by diverting the large subsidies it had been providing for the construction of railways into the war effort. As a result, real estate values in the city plummeted, and the population dropped as all the able-bodied men left to serve in the military.

Many pioneers have provided testimony of the economic devastation caused by the war to Prince George. "World War I killed the city. The money that was going to be spent here wasn't spent and the town died," said pioneer resident Jane Kennedy.

Another pioneer resident, Charles Olds, Sr., used these words to describe the scene on Third Avenue after World War I had put an end to the real estate boom:

I remember sitting on the sidewalk in Prince George with my brother-in-law who had a drugstore at that time. That's all he had, just a drugstore and no customers. None. We sat on the sidewalk eating chocolates out of his store. There was absolutely no sign of life, not a man or a chicken or anything on the whole street which is now Third Avenue.

Soon newspapers contained front page reports of the major battles being fought in Europe and the names of enlisted men from the area as they left to go to training camps elsewhere.

At home the citizens rallied behind the war effort by purchasing war savings certificates for $21.50, $43, and $86, which were redeemable in three years for $25, $50, and $100 respectively. Students and adults were also urged to make donations to the Belgian Relief Fund, the Prisoners of War fund, and the Red Cross, and to assist the wives and families left behind by the enlisted men. Women were also urged to knit socks, scarves, and balaclavas for the Red Cross to send to the soldiers.

EPIDEMICS STRIKE
The economic depression in Prince George following the outbreak of World War I was not the only hardship suffered by the residents of the

The "Fort George Boys," serving with the 62nd Battalion in 1915, posed for this formal photograph during their basic training in Vernon. Courtesy, Provicial Archives of British Columbia

three Georges during the first two decades of this century. Illness and epidemics were other ever-present threats.

The lack of a community health program meant that there was no one to ensure the safety of the community's water and food supplies or its garbage and human waste handling systems, nor was there an immunization program to protect citizens from diseases such as small pox, measles, and diphtheria. Early newspapers contained reports of the tragic deaths of young and old alike from diseases such as cholera and typhoid.

Typhoid is an often-fatal disease traceable to germ-infected food and drinking water. Consider then the inadequacy of the advice given to residents of the three Georges printed in a 1913 edition of the *Fort George Herald*: "Excess in eating and drinking, want of sleep and too much mental work predisposes persons to the onset of typhoid."

In a primitive attempt to prevent the contamination of wells each spring when water flooded over parts of the community, carrying with it the half-rotted garbage and manure that had accumulated during the winter, readers were further advised to clear all debris from their property and drench the soil with disinfectant.

In the early part of 1918 serious outbreaks of airborne diseases such as scarlet fever and whooping cough also took their toll on the community.

By September of that year there was growing concern about the epidemic of Spanish flu sweeping across North America. By mid-October the first cases of the dread disease were reported in the city and soon the limited medical facilities—small private nursing homes in Prince George and South Fort George and a small hospital on the Fort George townsite—proved to be totally inadequate to meet the needs of the disease-stricken residents. The situation was made worse by the number of seriously ill people flooding into the city from the logging camps along the rail line east of the city.

By October 18, 1918, all public meeting places including schools, theatres, and poolrooms were ordered to close in an effort to control the spread of the Spanish flu, and the Connaught Hotel on the southwest corner of Queensway and Second Avenue had been converted into a 15-bed emergency hospital.

Two days later it was reported there were more than 100 cases of the disease requiring medical attention in the community. The lack of trained nurses was overcome by assigning members of the provincial police force to work in the hospitals, and by calling on housewives to care for those who were most seriously ill. Soon Police Chief Dolan and Assistant Police Chief Graham were afflicted with the disease, as were the majority of the staff of the Grand Trunk Pacific Railway.

Dr. Eddie Lyon also became ill, leaving Dr. Lazier, who had recently

In 1920 stern-wheelers beached near South Fort George were damaged by local flooding. Courtesy, Provincial Archives of British Columbia

been released from a military hospital, to carry on alone.

On October 22 the Union Rooming House on East Third Avenue was transformed into a hospital for 30 patients, and on October 25 *The Citizen* reported that the Millar Addition School near Queensway and 15th Avenue had been converted into an emergency hospital for another 30 patients.

By October 29 the epidemic appeared to be subsiding. Twenty-one people were reported to have died—six of them Prince George residents. Sixty-two people remained in the hospitals and 10 percent of them were reported to be gravely ill.

Another problem arose when the community's only undertaker, J.W. Sandford, left for Victoria. His assistant, Dick Corless, had no training. But Sandford had left his textbooks behind and, after studying these, Corless became the town's undertaker.

Corless' son, John, said his mother told him that during the flu epidemic she went out to the shed behind the house to get some wood and found 14 bodies there. He recalled:

It was dark with no light and there 14 waiting burial. They had no one to dig the graves. I said to her, "Well, weren't you afraid?" and she said, "I'll tell you something John, it is not the dead that you gotta worry about it is the live ones."

When Dr. Carl Ewert was appointed the city's first medical health officer in 1940, working with public health nurse Eileen Snowden, he began an immunization program for schoolchildren and took steps to reduce water- and food-borne diseases.

By the 1940s polio was the most commonly reported communicable disease in the area and, until the Salk polio vaccine became available in 1955, during each summer it was a constant threat to the life and health of Prince George residents. During the outbreaks the only preventive measures residents could take were to get plenty of rest and stay away from public gatherings.

In 1954 when the population of the area served by the Northern Interior Health Unit had reached 36,000, Prince George was the first city in B.C. to introduce fluoride into its drinking water as a means of preventing dental cavities. But the health news was not all good. In 1958 the city was reported to have the third-highest rate of venereal disease in B.C.

During the 1960s there was an influx of people into the area due to the construction and start-up of the pulp mills. Many of these people built or purchased homes in the subdivisions which had sprung up in the unorganized areas around the periphery of the city. The lack of sewer and water systems in some of these areas resulted in infectious hepatitis becoming an endemic health problem.

In 1964 the city was hit by another flu epidemic which filled the hospital with seriously ill patients, forcing the hospital staff to declare a medical emergency.

FIRE: A CONSTANT THREAT

In addition to epidemics, the early residents of Prince George had another constant worry: fire.

A combination of poorly insulated wooden buildings heated by roaring wood fires and inadequate firefighting equipment meant fire was a constant threat, particularly during the winter months.

A list of some of the major fires which occurred in Prince George during the first two decades of this century will provide insight into the dimensions of the problem:

• July 1, 1911—It is believed that a careless smoker or a lamp or candle placed too close to a flimsy wall on the upper floor of the three-storey Hotel Northern started a fire which reduced the building to ashes. The threat of additional fires was imminent when the blaze sent a shower of sparks spewing over nearby wooden buildings. Hand-held fire extinguishers, bucket brigades, and wet blankets placed over nearby buildings were the only firefighting methods available. While the fire blazed in the upper part of the hotel, volunteers removed as much furniture and other valuables as they could from the lower floors. Unfortunately they were joined by looters who were carrying armloads of liquor out of the barroom. Not content with that, they also looted dresser drawers, picked the pockets of the firemen's discarded jackets, and stole the drawer in which the hotel's valuables had been placed. But the looters'

These buildings on the east side of George Street, between Third and Fourth Avenues, were destroyed by a fire which broke out in the basement of Hood's Limited on January 12, 1916. Courtesy, Bev Christensen

luck ended there because they took an envelope containing only the hotel's insurance papers and left behind two nondescript envelopes containing more than $1,000.

• December 11, 1913—A fire destroyed the Alamo Theatre and Nechaco General Stores at the corner of Central Avenue and Hammond Street in the Fort George townsite. The blaze is believed to have started in the unattended theatre when the creosote in a long, horizontal metal pipe chimney caught on fire. The intense heat of the blaze melted the pipe, spewing burning creosote onto the floor.

• January 7, 1914—A fire seriously damaged the roof of J.W. Scott's Hotel in the Fort George townsite.

• June 5, 1914—Two men, Bert Moody and an Austrian identified only as Sokolowsky, died in a fire at the Palace Rooms in South Fort George. There were 18 guests in the rooming house at the time.

• August 31, 1914—A fire broke out in the Prince George Restaurant and spread to the adjoining St. Regis Hotel on George Street. Both buildings were burned to the ground.

• November 13, 1914—One person died in a fire which destroyed the northernmost block of Central Avenue in the Fort George townsite. An explosion was heard before the fire erupted in the Fort George Hotel. The remains of victim Dick Spence, a steam shovel operator, were found in the ashes. Twelve other buildings were destroyed in the blaze.

• December 15, 1914—Fraser Rooms on Fourth Street in South Fort George was seriously damaged by a fire.

• December 26, 1914—Three adjacent buildings on Third Street in South Fort George comprising Robart's Hotel, West Rooms, and the Gore & McGregor survey office were destroyed by fire. The conflagration was thought to have been the work of a pyromaniac who, while the community was fighting the fire that started in the Robart's Hotel, entered the Nahrwald Building on the corner of Third and Hamilton Street and started yet another blaze by setting fire to papers on top of a bed.

• January 3, 1915—A night watchman discovered a fire in the Empress Hotel on the corner of Fourth and Hamilton streets in South Fort George. Despite the use of the community's new chemical firefighting equipment which had to be pulled to the scene of the fire by hand, the building was totally destroyed. Within a few days one company which had been selling fire insurance in the area, Empire Insurance, announced it was cancelling all fire policies in South Fort George.

• January 12, 1916—A fire broke out in the basement of Hood's Ltd., a general merchandise store, and destroyed all the buildings on the east side of George Street between Third and Fourth avenues.

• November 23, 1916—Another serious fire broke out on the east side of George Street, between Fourth and Fifth avenues, threatening Fort George Drugs and the Ritts-Kifer Hall. The buildings were saved but suffered extensive water damage.

FLOOD: A RECURRING PROBLEM
Ironically, during this same period in the history of Prince George,

property in other parts of the city was being destroyed by floods caused by heavy runoffs in the Nechako and Fraser rivers during the spring. Flooding was also taking a toll during the winter, when ice jams formed in the Nechako River as it flowed between the small islands near its junction with the Fraser River, creating natural dams.

These floods, particularly in the area of Cottonwood Island Park, seem to have been such a regular occurrence the early newspapers made little mention of them. But pictures remain of the floodings that occurred in 1917, 1920, 1934, 1936, 1937, and 1939.

Pioneer resident Arthur Fisk reported his memories of the flood which occurred in 1921. He said the ice backed up to the deck of the first wooden bridge over the Nechako River, which had been completed in November 1916. The ice posed such a threat to the bridge, located slightly downstream from the present bridge, that it was replaced in 1931 by one that stood higher above the river on solid cement and rock footings.

Fisk noted that the huge ice dam forced the water to flow over Cottonwood Island Park, onto the rail yards and First Avenue, from its eastern edge to its junction with Queensway. Water also rose in the vicinity of City Hall and between Fifth and Seventh avenues. He went on to say:

This motorized firetruck was a valuable addition to the city's equipment in the early 1900s. Prior to its purchase, firefighters either pulled the equipment to the site of the fire themselves, or used a horse-drawn carriage. Courtesy, Provincial Archives of British Columbia

On the other side of the Nechako River there was a family living in a house on the bank of the river . . . It was 50 below zero and his wife was standing on the top of the roof all night. She screamed and the police heard her and went over and rescued her.

In his report to the superintendent of the provincial police commission, Police Chief Thomas W.S. Parsons provided this report of the flood which occurred in 1933:

On the night of the 19th heavy ice jams at the confluence of the Fraser and Nechaco [sic] Rivers, near Prince George, caused flooding of the lower sections of the city. Thereupon, handicapped by a blizzard and with the temperature at 25 below zero, police and citizens worked valiantly and successfully to rescue some 26 persons who were not only isolated but in some personal danger.

Flooding continued in the vicinity of Cottonwood Island Park until the mid-seventies, when the city moved the remaining residents out of the area. By this time the flow of the Nechako River had also been reduced by the construction of the Kenney Dam.

DEPRESSION PARALYZES THE COMMUNITY

The economy of Prince George and its surrounding area was stagnant throughout the period between World War I and World War II. Residents were preoccupied with trying to reestablish their lives after the disruption caused by World War I and, later, the crash of the New York stock

In 1921 an ice jam backed up to the deck of the first bridge built across the Nechako River. This bridge, which was slightly downstream from the present Cameron Street bridge, had a swing-span that enabled stern-wheelers to make their way up the river to the Fort George townsite and beyond. Courtesy, Provincial Archives of British Columbia

market on October 29, 1929. Because information flowed into the area slowly, the crash was summarized two days after it happened in 16 lines near the bottom of the first page of *The Citizen*. In another brief story printed in the same paper, Prime Minister Mackenzie King reassured residents by saying the Canadian economy had never been more sound.

In November 1929 King visited Prince George as part of a whistle-stop tour of Western Canada. During his speech he spoke only of the government's success in reducing Canada's war debts concurrent with reducing taxation, and said nothing about the growing concern over a depression.

In a campaign speech during the federal election held on July 31, 1930, John Fraser, the Conservative candidate for M.P. in the federal riding of Cariboo, said the Liberal government's policy of reducing trade tariffs was responsible for the large number of people who could not find work in the area. Liberal candidate Harry Perry ran on the government's record of reducing debt and taxes.

Fraser was elected to Prime Minister Richard B. Bennett's Conservative government by a majority of 373 votes. The Conservative's victory was ascribed to the Liberal government's refusal to provide employment relief grants to the provinces.

The first sign of employment problems in Prince George appeared in July 1930 when *The Citizen* reported that a lack of markets had forced the closure of two mills located east of Prince George—the Gale and Trick Mill at Aleza Lake and the Eagle Lake Spruce Mill at Giscome.

On October 16, 1930, John Fraser, M.P. for Cariboo, came to the city to explain the federal government's plans for the $900,000 approved for em-

In 1921, near the east end of First Avenue, an ice jam in the Nechako River sent water spilling across Cottonwood Island Park, onto the railway yards, across the street, and into the old riverbed that lies to the north of Patricia Boulevard. Courtesy, Provincial Archives of British Columbia

ployment relief in B.C. *The Citizen* reported that Fraser told local businessmen:

There would doubtless be cases of applicants for relief who had enjoyed the advantage of employment during the summer, but now having squandered their earnings, would be active in striving for a share of the relief vote. Such people should not be given consideration in advance of those who had been without employment during the greater part of the summer.

By October 30, 1930, *The Citizen* reported that 271 men were out of work in the small communities between Prince George and McBride, and 385 men were out of work in the City of Prince George. The population of Prince George was reported to have been 3,500. The number of people unemployed in the surrounding area was probably higher because no reports had been received from McBride, Dome Creek, or Aleza Lake.

On November 20, 1930, Rolf Bruhn, B.C.'s Minister of Public Works, informed the city it would receive a minimum of $20,000 to pay two-thirds of the cost of "feeding the destitute."

But Mayor Alex Patterson was concerned about the number of "floaters" the city would be responsible for feeding. These were men from all across Canada who had been riding the rails and dropped off in Prince George seeking a free meal. As the Depression deepened, every town along the rail line had a community of these unemployed drifters living in a hobo jungle nearby. Prince George was no exception. Floaters were reported to be living in what is now Cottonwood Island Park.

The city council considered a number of work projects for these relief workers, including construction of a trail to the top of Connaught Hill to the newly constructed ski jump and toboggan slide, raising the grade of George Street near its south end, shoring up the railway ties used to support the roadway on the south side of Third Avenue between Quebec and Brunswick streets, and filling in the area in front of City Hall to the level of George Street. The provincial and federal govern-

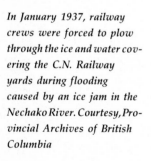

In January 1937, railway crews were forced to plow through the ice and water covering the C.N. Railway yards during flooding caused by an ice jam in the Nechako River. Courtesy, Provincial Archives of British Columbia

ments provided half of the funding for relief employment by matching any monies a municipality put into these projects. One of the requirements for these grants was that there be no equipment employed on the projects.

When it became apparent employment relief was going to be required for many years, the senior levels of government decided it would require those receiving relief payments to work on the building of highways. The first approved highway construction plan was for a road between Prince George and the Alberta border.

Soon relief camps had been established at Penny, Dome Creek, and McBride. The men were provided with food, shelter, and clothing, and paid 20 cents per day. But conditions in the camps were reported to be horrendous and men began drifting back to Prince George bearing tales of poor food, lack of medical care, and disorganization, which kept them sitting idly in the camps.

To relieve the situation in Prince George, unmarried, destitute, and homeless men receiving direct relief from the city were ordered to go to the camps to work. A delegation of the men appeared before the city council bearing a petition protesting the order. It had been signed by many people, including businessmen who were concerned they would lose the business the relief dollars provided if the men were forced to leave the city. Still, early in 1931 the federal government announced the money it had allocated for employment relief was exhausted and the city was forced to halt all relief payments by the first week of April.

Throughout the Depression municipal and provincial governments split the cost of providing relief for single people, and the cost of providing relief to married persons was split three ways between the federal, provincial, and municipal governments.

Soon the city council was told the city was spending $900 to $1,000 a week providing direct relief for the floaters who received 40 cents a day for food and 25 cents for a bed. The relief money provided to married men varied according to their number of dependents.

Throughout the 1930s the threat of having their meagre employment relief payments cut off hung over the heads of unemployed men and their families, either because the city could no longer pay them or because it was decided they were not eligible for relief.

The situation of the relief workers continued to worsen throughout the 1930s. Evidence of the increasing distress among the elderly and unemployed was found in the numerous reports of suicides and attacks—even murders—that occurred in the area during the period.

On November 16, 1933, four men—Charles Peterson, Ole Olson, Ragnor Lindal, and David Dickerson—were charged with attacking Constable William Smith during a demonstration by 75 men at the Government Building at the southwest intersection of Third Avenue and Brunswick Street.

On March 15, 1934, a delegation of relief workers appeared before the city council with a petition bearing 960 signatures, calling for a uniform scale of relief, a national employment insurance scheme, and more meaningful work in the city. In addition they demanded a minimum of five days' work per month for single men, eight days' work per month for a family of two, and one extra day's work per month per each additional dependent in a family of more than two people. They also wanted to be paid

In 1934, relief workers and their wives march along the 1200 block of Third Avenue during a May Day Parade in protest to the amount of relief pay they were receiving during The Depression. Courtesy, Prince George Public Library

50 cents an hour for an eight-hour day and have all relief payments paid in cash instead of the "humiliating and degrading script system" in which they were given a voucher that could be cashed at a local business. Finally, they wanted the charges against Peterson, Olson, Lindal, and Dickerson dropped.

Although the men did not get everything they wanted, they did gain one concession: the pay for single men was increased to 50 cents an hour.

When a jury found Lindal not guilty of attacking the policeman, the charges against the three remaining men were dropped. The decision was based on the jury's belief that the men had a right to be in the government office because it was a public place, and the fact that there was no proof that a policeman's duties included clearing people out of the government agent's office.

However, the unrest among the unemployed was not eliminated, and on May 13, 1935, 40 to 50 striking relief workers clashed with 7 provincial police near the Grand Trunk Pacific Railway bridge. The policemen were guarding four truckloads of relief workers travelling to work on the highway between Prince George and Quesnel. They were attacked as they attempted to remove a barricade which the relief strikers had erected across the highway in an effort to prevent the men from going to work for less than 50 cents an hour.

The police fired a few warning shots in the air before the strikers fell upon them with clubs and rocks, breaking one policeman's arm and inflicting severe head injuries to another.

Of the four men arrested following the fracas, Heitman Johnson was found guilty of three charges of assault and sentenced to 18 months in jail, and Jack Rutledge, Frederick Barker, and Gus Edvall were found guilty of one charge of assault and sentenced to six months in jail.

WAR BRINGS NEW ACTIVITY

Ironically, relief from the misery of unemployment came in the form of more violence.

Although there had been reports of it for months, the first signs of World War II noticed by the residents of Prince George came late in August 1939, when Captain H. Angle arrived in the city with 30 men from the B.C. Dragoons to guard the Fraser River Railway bridge. The soldiers were part of the military preparations under way across Canada prior to the declaration of war against Germany on September 9, 1939.

By late August 1939 the young men of the community were being urged to join the Second Searchlight Battery of the Royal Canadian Artillery. The 30 to 50 men expected to enlist would be trained to defend Canada's Pacific Coast in the event of an attack by the Japanese. They would serve under the command of Lieutenant William Crocker of Prince George as part of a unit which had its headquarters in Prince Rupert. Crocker's subalterns were second lieutenants Lorne Swannell and Howard Alexander. By September 7, 1939, 20 men had joined up to form the nucleus of the unit and were holding regular drills outside the Royal Canadian Legion on the northwest corner of Fifth Avenue and Quebec Street.

On October 5 hundreds of residents gathered at the railway station to say goodbye to the first 30 men of the Second Searchlight Battery, who left for active duty in Prince Rupert.

An army camp for more than 6,000 men was constructed west of Central Street between 15th and 22nd, at the foot of Cranbrook Hill

Severe flooding occurred early in June 1936. The effects at the southwestern end of the Grand Trunk Pacific Railway bridge are seen here. Courtesy, Provincial Archives of British Columbia

(today Carter Industrial Area). The officers were housed on the bank above the Nechako between Carney and Central.

By this time the city was preparing to defend itself against a Japanese attack from the west. Men who were not eligible to join the armed forces volunteered to become members of the Pacific Coast Militia Rangers (PCMR), a corps of volunteer citizens being trained to protect the city against invasion. Air raid practices were held, in which residents were required to ensure there were no lights shining from their houses and corps of Red Cross workers and PCMR volunteers patrolled the streets until the all-clear siren sounded.

Everyone, including children, was caught up in the war effort. War bond drives were held. Residents were encouraged to collect aluminum wrappers from chewing gum and cigarettes from which metal could be extracted for war use. Gasoline, tires, sugar, and meat were rationed, and children were urged to create more food for the soldiers by planting "victory gardens."

When residents heard reports of Japanese submarines being sighted off the B.C. coast and rumors of Japanese troops landing on the Alaskan Panhandle, all enemy aliens were rounded up and removed from the vicinity of the city.

Unlike World War I, which left the city slowly sliding into a depression, World War II signalled the start of an economic boom for the area. When Great Britain and Europe began rebuilding their shattered cities, the demand for lumber rose and hundreds of small mills began sawing up the rich harvest of spruce trees which carpeted B.C.'s entire central-interior plateau.

Accompanied by children, a contingent of Pacific Coast Militia Rangers march past the 1300 block of Third Avenue during the parade held on Labor Day 1942. Courtesy, Fraser-Fort George Regional Museum

*Previous page: Two local
horses pose for the camera.
Photo by Bob Clarke*

*Right: Fort George Park is
seen here in the stillness of
dawn. Photo by Bob Clarke*

90

Bottom left and far left: Autumn splendor abounds in Connaught Hill Park. Photo by Bob Clarke

Below: Forests For The World is located northwest of Prince George proper. Photo by Bob Clarke

Above: The productivity of agricultural land in Prince George is evident. These stooks of grain were photographed on Cranbook Hill. Courtesy, Mary Fallis

Left: This local vegetable grower poses with his produce. Photo by Bob Clarke

Facing page: These sheep flock together in the warm autumn sun. Photo by Bob Clarke

Above: A team of horses strains to pull a load during The Exhibition, a local fair and agricultural show. The very first exhibition was held in 1912, and has since been an annual event, with the exception of 1914, when it was cancelled due to the outbreak of World War I. Courtesy, Dave Milne

Right: The Industrial Forestry Service Ltd. was founded in 1952. Here at the Ness Lake Forest Nursery, both container and transplant stock are produced. Photo by Bob Clarke

Jogging provides this local resident with a sound mind and body. Photo by Bob Clarke

Above: These young Beavers held a meeting in Fort George Park. Photo by Bob Clarke

Right: Golfing is a favorite pastime of many local residents. Photo by Bob Clarke

The Northern Hardware store provides the time of day for passersby. Photo by Bob Clarke

An artisan of the Prince George Potter's Guild presents local work. Photo by Bob Clarke

Local firefighters practice drills regularly. Photo by Bob Clarke

Above: The Prince George Pulp Mill rises above the Grand Trunk Pacific Railway bridge. Photo by Bob Clarke

Right: The greater Prince George Visitors and Convention Bureau is an available resource for tourists and locals alike. Photo by Bob Clarke

Above: This modern City Hall of Prince George was constructed in the very same locale as the first Prince George City Hall. Photo by Bob Clarke

Left: Prince George Public Library houses thousands of volumes for both pleasure and research. Photo by Bob Clarke

Above: Prince George Regional Hospital is well respected within the community. Photo by Bob Clarke

Right: Fort George Regional Museum contributes much to the local art community. Photo by Bob Clarke

Facing page: The city of Prince George is graced with a crescent moon at twilight. Photo by Bob Clarke

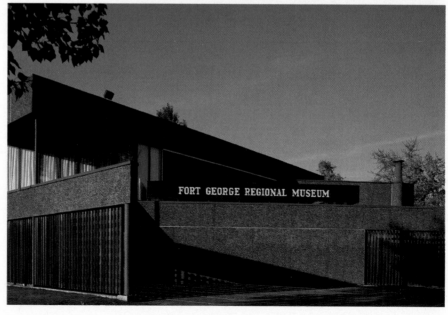

*This crew of men, at the Sinclair
Spruce Mill, pose during
mealtime. Courtesy, Provincial
Archives of British Columbia*

VII

INDUSTRY ARRIVES

. . . Fort George will not be a mere town—it will be a city—the second largest city in British Columbia—a city situated much like Spokane, with more and greater natural advantages than Edmonton, Saskatoon or Calgary.
—B.C. Bulletin of Information, March 1911

This 1911 prediction finally came true more than 70 years after it was made, following the second major influx of people into the area.

Unlike the early part of the century, when settlers were attracted to Prince George by the promise of cheap land and construction opportunities, it was the lumber industry and the building of three pulp mills on the banks of the Fraser River that lured money and people during this second period of population expansion.

During the time between the prediction in 1911 and a prediction in 1965 that Prince George would have a population of 200,000 by the turn of the century, the city's economic dependence on the lumber industry resulted in a series of boom and bust periods. When lumber prices rose, everyone prospered; when lumber prices fell, everyone suffered. In 1946 and 1953, woodworkers' strikes crippled the economy of the city of Prince George.

RAILWAYS SPARK ECONOMIC BOOM

At the beginning of the nineteenth century, the construction of the Grand Trunk Pacific Railway set off the city's first boom. While the railway was being built the city's population grew rapidly, services improved, and building lots sold at inflated prices. Everyone was convinced that the city was destined to become a major metropolis. Some said it would be as important as Chicago.

Whenever the boom appeared to be losing momentum, it was refueled by stories of gold strikes on the outskirts of the city, word of another railway being planned for the area, and other promises of future greatness found in a series of newspaper articles and brochures advertising land values of the area.

In one of these brochures George Hammond, the ubiquitous promoter of the Fort George townsite, predicted:

Just as in ancient times "all roads led to Rome," so all present and future railroads in central British Columbia lead to Fort George. Their builders cannot evade or

Above: The well-stocked shelves of Leith Brothers Hardware, which once stood on the northwest corner of Third Avenue and George Street, give mute testimony to the volume of business transacted circa 1920. Courtesy, Fraser-Fort George Regional Museum

A marked improvement of shopping facilities has been noted since 1965, when the construction of this shopping complex at the intersection of 15th Avenue and Victoria Street began. Courtesy, Fraser-Fort George Regional Museum

escape this, for it is due to a natural condition. The topography of the country makes it impossible for them to do otherwise.

At first it appeared Hammond was correct, for during the first two decades of this century there were reports of 19 different railways being planned to crisscross the river valley now occupied by Prince George.

Only two railways were actually completed.

In 1902 Charles Hays proposed that the federal government should subsidize construction of the Grand Trunk Pacific Railway. It was to run from Winnipeg through the Yellowhead Pass in the Rockies and from Fort George to Kaien Island at the mouth of the Skeena River. It had just been completed when, in March 1916, it went into receivership. The federal government turned the operation of the railway over to the Canadian National Railway on January 30, 1923.

Vancouver businessmen had become concerned about the amount of business that would flow toward Edmonton when the Grand Trunk Pacific Railway was completed. No doubt they had also heard the predictions that Prince George was going to grow into a large city, and wanted to ensure they obtained their share of the business from the new city.

They succeeded in catching the ear of Premier Richard McBride. In 1912 he announced that his government was going to build the Pacific and Great Eastern Railway (PGE), from North Vancouver along the east side of the Fraser River through Fort George and on to the Peace River.

After many political promises and false starts, the PGE railway to Prince George was finally completed 40 years later. The first official train arrived in Prince George on November 1, 1952. By this time the railway's quaint passenger cars, heated by a coal stove at each end, had been replaced by modern coaches. But the PGE's nicknames—Prince George Eventually, Please Go Easy, Past God's Endurance, and Premier's Great 'Eadache—lingered on. In 1958 the rail line was completed to the Peace River community of Little Prairie, now known as Chetwynd. The PGE was renamed the British Columbia Railway on April 1, 1972. Its name was changed again on June 19, 1984, to BC Rail Ltd.

During the first decade of this century construction was begun on another railway to Prince George. The Edmonton, Dunvegan and B.C. Railway was to travel north from Edmonton to Dunvegan, near Grande Prairie, then along the Peace and Parsnip rivers and through the Pine Pass to Prince George. An alternate route was designated from Dunvegan to Hudson's Hope, then to Fort McLeod, Giscome Portage, and Prince George. A branch line was proposed to run from Fort McLeod to the Yukon.

The rail line was never finished. But the more than 300 miles of line north of Edmonton that had been completed before construction was halted by the outbreak of World War I are now used by the Northern Alberta Railway.

There were also reports of five other rail lines through the Fort George area. These railway lines were only mentioned in the *Fort George Herald*, owned by George Hammond. Therefore, it is possible they consisted of nothing more than conversations between Hammond and other ambitious promoters bent on making money by selling shares in nonexistent railways. These railway proposals were:

• *The B.C. and Dawson Railway, which was to follow a route from Fort George through the Pine Pass to Dunvegan, where it would connect with the Pacific and Hudson's Bay Railway, and the Edmonton, Yukon and Pacific Railway being proposed for construction in northern Alberta.*

• *The B.C. and Alaska Railway to run from Quesnel through Fort George to a point west of Vanderhoof, then north to Alaska, reported in the* Fort George Herald *on September 17, 1910, as being planned by Jean Wolkenstein of New York.*

• *The Cariboo, Barkerville and Willow River Railway Company, which the December 7, 1912, edition of the* Fort George Herald *reported as having applied to Parliament for permission to build a rail line from a point on the Grand Trunk Pacific near Eagle Lake to the gold-mining city of Barkerville.*

• *The Pacific and Hudson's Bay Railway, from Bella Coola northeast through Fort George to the Peace River country and Hudson's Bay, was being considered by the federal government according to the* Fort George Herald *of February 15, 1913.*

• *The Pacific, Peace River and Athabasca Railway to run from the Pacific Ocean near the mouth of the Nass River across country, through Prince George and the Parsnip and Peace river valleys to Fort McMurray and Prince Albert, was reported as planned for construction in the* Fort George Herald *on November 22, 1913.*

No formal proposals were submitted for the nine other rail lines rumored to be in the works for the area around Fort George. Some of them may have been the original names for proposals later made under other company names. Others may also have been figments of Hammond's imagination. The names of these proposals were:

• *The Ashcroft, Barkerville and Fort George Railway, shown on an early map running along the east side of the Fraser River from Ashcroft north to Barkerville and Prince George.*

• *The Pacific, Northern and Omineca Railway.*

• *The Edmonton, Yukon and Pacific Railway.*

• *The Vancouver, Westminster Northern and Yukon Railway, which was to have used the same route the PGE took from Lillooet to Quesnel.*

• *The Pine Pass Railway, which may have been a portion of the proposed PGE railway north from Prince George to the Peace River.*

• *The Victoria and Fort George Railway.*

• *The Portland Canal Shortline Railroad.*

• *The Bella Coola and Dunvegan Railway.*

• *The Pacific and Nechaco [sic] Valley Railway.*

The railway construction boom was not unique to Prince George. When it was over, the B.C. government passed a bill officially declaring the end of more than 200 inactive railway construction proposals.

Following the outbreak of World War I, the railway construction boom at Prince George turned into a bust. Real estate prices dropped, leaving residents and speculators holding property purchased at inflated prices and businesses for which there were few customers.

LUMBER MARKETS DEVELOP

There was one bright spot in the economy. The completion of the Grand Trunk Pacific Railway gave locally produced lumber access to eastern markets. By 1919 the Prince George Board of Trade reported there were 18 sawmills operating between Prince George and McBride. Most of the 33 million board feet produced that year was exported to the Prairies. It was almost three times as much as the 12 million board feet produced in 1915, the first year records were kept in the Prince George Forest District.

Cliff Husband drives a four-horse team, pulling a load of logs, at a logging camp east of Prince George. Courtesy, Cliff Husband

This aerial view of Prince George from The Cutbanks, before the arrival of the pulp mills, shows one of many beehive burners that once lined the south bank of the Nechako River, the railway roundhouse and water tower, and, in the background, the old City Hall and Fire Hall. Courtesy, Sophie Partridge

A load of logs is moved cautiously along the plank road used by the first loggers in the area of Prince George circa 1950. Courtesy, Fraser-Fort George Regional Museum

The first hint of the economic potential of the pulp industry came in 1920, when a company known as the Fraser River Syndicate contacted the B.C. government with a proposal to construct a pulp and paper mill and sawmill complex near Prince George. The pulp mill was to be capable of producing 100 tons per day, and the sawmill complex was to put out 100,000 to 125,000 board feet per day. To provide the timber for these ventures, the company wanted pulp license reserves on 175 square miles of land along the Fraser River and its tributaries east of Prince George.

During the first phase of the project the syndicate planned to spend more than $3 million to develop the pulp and lumber mills and provide the required hydro-electric energy. In the second phase, another $3 million would be spent expanding production to include 120 tons of newsprint and 50 tons of kraft paper per day.

In October 1921 the B.C. government set a price of 93 cents per cord as the stumpage and royalty the company would pay for its timber. In today's terms it is the equivalent of 73 cents a cunit or 25.7 cents a cubic meter.

The government balked when the syndicate then demanded the royalty be fixed at that price for 30 years. In 1924 the government introduced a new Royalty Act which partially met the syndicate's needs for longer tenure.

But it was too late. By this time one of the major investors in the project, Robert Tyhurst, had been murdered while he was working in the office of the St. Maurice Paper Co. in Joliette, Quebec, and another investor, F.P. Jones of Montreal, had become ill. Falling lumber and pulp prices also meant the proposed mills were no longer viable. The syndicate went into receivership in 1932 and Prince George had to wait more than 30 years before "the smell of money" drifted over the city from the three pulp mills that had been constructed nearby.

Until the opening of the first pulp mill in 1966, the city's economy was so dependent on the lumber industry that the annual records of lumber production in the area reflected the economic conditions existing in the area.

THE AGE OF AIR TRAVEL

During the first four decades of this century, the railway to Prince Rupert and Edmonton, and the gravel roads south to Cache Creek en route to Vancouver and west to Prince Rupert, were the main transportation routes into Prince George. The age of air travel arrived in 1920, when four planes flying on an expedition from New York to Nome landed on Central Avenue. Virginia Johnson, daughter of pioneer hotelier J.H. Johnson, said residents lengthened and widened Central Avenue in preparation for the arrival of the planes.

A fully serviced airport was not available in Prince George until March 1940, when the Prince George Airport was opened on the bench of land east of the Fraser River. It was built by the city with federal assistance and on the recommendation of the United States-Canada Defense Board, as one in a string of defense airports in central B.C.

Ten years later Prince George entered a decade of intense development. It began in 1952 with the official opening of the John Hart Highway, which finally gave the city access to the Peace River area. The network of highways which resulted in the city being nicknamed the

Prince George Annual Lumber Production 1920-1940

Bd.ft.

1920 - 38 million - Postwar reconstruction creates a demand for lumber. Prices rise to $32 per thousand for rough lumber and $38 per thousand for planed lumber.

1921 - 22 million - Demand falls when Prairie farmers begin to feel the pinch of the Depression.

1922 - 25 million - The economy remains stagnant.

1923 - 37 million - The economy of B.C. improves slightly.

1924 - 70 million - The lifting of an embargo makes it possible to ship lumber to Eastern Canada and the U.S.

1925 - 70 million - When fires destroy the Grain Growers mill at Hutton and the Allan-Thrasher mill at Snowshoe, the district is unable to increase its production.

1926 - 100 million- The Grain Growers and Allan-Thrasher mills are rebuilt and back into production.

1927 - 74 million - Mill owners miscalculate demand for lumber during the summer and fail to get enough logs out of the bush during the winter logging season.

1928 - 160 million- More logs are removed during the winter and demand continues high during the summer.

1931 - 24 million - Sawmills are closed by the onset of the Depression. Hundreds of men are thrown out of work.

1932 - 15 million - Lowest lumber production in the district since 1915.

1939 - 53 million - The outbreak of World War II creates a demand for B.C. lumber.

1940 - 73 million - Logging is declared an essential industry

Above: On June 2, 1937, the first planes carrying air mail arrived in Prince George. This was regarded as considerable advancement for a community that, 30 years before, had received its mail by sternwheeler. Courtesy, Fraser-Fort George Regional Museum

Below: Crowds gathered when these U.S. bombers landed on the small airfield located near the junction of highways 16 and 97 during World War II. Courtesy, Fraser-Fort George Regional Museum

"Hub of the North" was completed in 1968, when the Yellowhead Highway was completed to Jasper.

Spurred by the activity in the lumber industry north of the city, the population grew rapidly, yet there was little housing available for the new residents. In 1950, to meet the demand for building lots, the provincial government began selling the sites surveyed as part of the Fort George townsite west of Carney Street during the first decade of this century. The land had reverted to the Crown when the grandiose plans for Fort George fell apart.

Many of the people buying these lots found they were served by neither roads nor streetlights, and the water for their household needs had to be carried from public taps along Fifth Avenue. In most cases the posts from the earlier surveys had disappeared. Therefore many of the new property owners took the quickest route to locating their property line and just stepped off their lot allotment from the nearest landmark. Sometimes this was nothing more than the spot determined by other landowners who also had stepped off their property.

As a result, when the land was resurveyed after it was taken into the city, it was found that some homes were sitting partially on neighboring property.

In 1954 Mayor Gordon Bryant led a delegation of city officials to Victoria to complain that the provincial government was pocketing all the money from the sale of the lots west of Carney Street, while the city was forced to bear the cost of providing water and roads to the rapidly developing area.

According to City Manager Chester Jeffrey, the two sides reached a land-development agreement which set the stage for the city to control land prices and subdivision development. Under the terms of the agreement, the city received one lot for every three lots sold by the provincial government. The money the city received from the sale of its lots was placed in a reserve fund to later be used to develop and sell fully serviced subdivisions.

According to Jeffrey, there were many complaints about the city entering into the real estate development business. But by developing and releasing fully serviced lots according to demand, the city council was able to ensure that Prince George developed in an orderly manner according to a plan developed by architect Desmond Parker. The plan provided for small, self-contained subdivisions which included community schools, parks, and a mixture of single-family dwellings, duplexes, and apartments.

Development was not so easily controlled in the unregulated areas surrounding the city, where many of the city's new residents were building their own homes.

The ribbon of land along Hart Highway and Highway 97 South developed in a helter-skelter manner, in which property owners and real estate developers subdivided and sold property. This came to be known as the "ribbon development." At first each home had its own well and septic systems. Soon, however, there were reports of wells being contaminated by the sewage systems. The need for a safer water supply led to the formation of water improvement districts in these areas.

GROWTH PUTS PRESSURE ON SCHOOLS
The more than 800 small lumber mills operating in the area during the early 1950s also created a problem for the school district, which had a policy of providing a school wherever there were 10 or more school-age children. To meet the demand for small schools near the sawmills, the district began constructing portable school buildings which could be moved onto the mill sites.

Bob Gracey, secretary-treasurer of the school district from 1949 to

1967, said that when he began working for the district there were only two schools along the Hart Highway from the Nechako River to Salmon Valley.

The school population grew quickly, as most of the people moving into Prince George during the 1950s had young children. Soon the city was boasting that it had the highest birthrate outside of Calcutta, and rightfully so—B.C.'s vital statistics records for 1956 show that the City of Prince George had a birthrate of 54.2 per 1,000 residents, compared to the provincial average of 25.9.

By the late 1950s, talk of plans for the construction of a pulp mill in the area started speculation that the city was facing another economic boom.

The talk gained validity in May 1962, when Canadian Forest Products announced plans to spend $50 million to construct what later became known as Prince George Pulp and Paper on a large meander of the Fraser River at the confluence of the Fraser and Nechako rivers.

A propeller-driven plane taxies across the snowy runway toward the first airport terminal of Prince George Airport. Courtesy, Sophie Partridge

Right: Looking northwest from Connaught Hill in 1952, the Anglican church under construction on Seventh Avenue can be seen, as well as the government building, which stood at the intersection of Third Avenue and Brunswick Street. Courtesy, Provincial Archives of British Columbia

Above: The 400 block of George Street was photographed circa 1960, prior to the announcement of major industrial developments in the area. Courtesy, Fraser-Fort George Regional Museum

Construction began in 1964, and by the time the mill began producing pulp and paper in July 1966, two more pulp mills, Northwood Pulp and Intercontinental Pulp, were being built near Prince George.

The influx of construction workers created another housing crisis. Many were forced to live in motels, trailers, and substandard houses in the unorganized ribbon development areas along the highways. During 1966 *The Citizen* conducted a survey of 32 apartment complexes in the city without finding one vacancy.

In May 1966 Mayor Garvin Dezell estimated that 4,000 people had moved into the city the previous year. He said 2,000 new units would be required during the next two years to meet the housing demand. The situation became more desperate when the Central Mortgage and Housing Corporation (CMHC) decided to reduce the amount of mortgage money it provided to B.C.

Mayor Dezell met with Labor Minister Jack Nicholson and a representative of CMHC in an effort to head off the housing crisis in the city. Dezell pointed out that despite the decline in the demand for new homes elsewhere in Canada, Prince George needed an infusion of mortgage money to meet its growing need for housing. Before he left, Nicholson predicted CMHC would provide enough money to construct 500 units.

It was during this period that low-rental units were built near Upland Street and apartment complexes were built on 15th Avenue west of the Bypass Highway.

The Prince George Pulp Mill, seen here under construction in 1965, was the first mill built in the vicinity of Prince George. Courtesy, Fraser-Fort George Regional Museum

Another indication of the magnitude of the housing demand during this period was the speed with which the city's 400 fully serviced lots in Spruceland were gobbled up. When the city put the Lakewood, Perry, and Highglen subdivisons on the market in 1966, those building lots disappeared just as quickly.

If the city was hard-pressed to meet the demand for additional housing, the school district faced a herculean task in providing classroom space for all the new students.

In June 1966 the Ministry of Education at first rejected the district's plan to spend $3.8 million to construct Prince George Secondary School. School board chairman Jim Elliot pointed out that enrollment in the district was expected to increase by 2,200 students in September. Without the immediate availability of new schools, all of these students—the equivalent of more than 70 classrooms—would be forced to attend school in shifts. In fact, throughout the construction boom in the 1960s, many students received most of their public school education while attending either a morning shift or an afternoon shift at one of the district's overcrowded community schools. Eventually, however, the Prince George Secondary School was built, and it opened in February 1968.

In 1975 the city's boundaries were expanded to include the developed areas of Pineview and the areas along the Hart Highway and Highway 16 West.

In 1981, the first census taken following amalgamation showed that Prince George had, in fact, lived up to the prediction made in the March 1911 edition of the B.C. Bulletin, becoming the second-largest city in B.C. According to the 1981 census, B.C.'s five largest cities and their populations were: Vancouver, 414,281; Prince George, 67,559; Victoria, 64,379; Kamloops, 64,048; and Kelowna, 59,196.

The worldwide recession of the early 1980s brought the booming economy of the Prince George area to a sudden stop. The population growth stalled, interest rates skyrocketed to as high as 20 percent, and unemployment rates climbed. Faced with higher prices, individuals and businesses were forced to tighten their belts and trim their budgets in an effort to maintain their economic equilibrium.

During the 1980s Prince George residents also began welcoming a new type of work force into the community when, each spring, a small army of tree planters arrived in the area to begin the mammoth task of replanting the forests being harvested to feed the pulp mills and sawmills.

By 1988 the economy of Prince George and other communities in northern B.C. began to improve and plans were revived to extend the B.C. Railway northwest to Dease Lake to make it possible to harvest the timber resources of the area between Prince George and the Yukon border. This time, as part of the provincial Social Credit government's privatization plans, the northern development of the railway would be carried out with money from locally-owned private companies—Prince George Wood Preserving Ltd. and Rustad Bros. Co. Ltd.—and not with government grants as had been the case in the past.

As Prince George approached the 75th anniversary of its incorporation, a group of residents from the north central-interior of the province began promoting a proposal to have a university built as a means of stimulating and maintaining the region's economic development. Prince

George was proposed as the site of the main campus of the university of the north being proposed by the Interior University Society. The proposal put forth by the Interior University Society and its chairman, Murray Sadler, called for a university with 14 campuses and study centres scattered throughout a region extending from 100 Mile House to Fort Nelson and from the Queen Charlotte Islands to the Alberta border.

Another group of residents saw Prince George as the cultural and convention centre of northern British Columbia. They proposed that a centre to be known as Discovery Place—designed by world-class architect Arthur Erickson—be built in the city. The site chosen for the centre, on the west side of Connaught Hill, is near the site of the first city hall and the wooden ski jump which once had been on the hill.

Spurred by news of more industrial development in communities to the east and west of Prince George which would use the city as a distribution centre, and a proposal to build a large hydrogen peroxide plant in Prince George to serve the needs of pulp mills throughout Western Canada, by late in 1988 the residents of Prince George began putting the recession that had dominated most of the 1980s behind them. Today, as the city approaches its 75th anniversary in 1990, the people of Prince George can look to the future with optimism.

This vocational school was the forerunner of the College of New Caledonia. When it opened in September 1962, it offered courses in heavy-duty mechanics, auto mechanics, millwrighting, welding, commercial subjects, and practical nursing. The approximate cost of the building was $1.7 million. Courtesy, Provincial Archives of British Columbia

The first Presbyterian missionary in Fort George, the Reverend C. Melville Wright, left, posed for this photo during the second meeting of the Caribou Presbytery in Fort George. Courtesy, Provincial Archives of British Columbia.

VIII
PARTNERS
IN
PROGRESS

As the old B.X. Steamboat drew near to the banks of the Fraser River at South Fort George in May 1912, a kindly disposed, middle-aged Dakotan, with whom my wife and I had become acquainted on the journey said, "Don't get off the boat; go back to where you came from as quickly as you can. I'm not getting off, don't you, young man, for all this dog-garned country is good for is growing Christmas trees." We landed. Those trees are spruce, and today give employment directly and indirectly to many thousands in the area tributary to Prince George.

—Harry G. Perry, from the foreword to A History of Prince George *by the Reverend F.E. Runnals*

Prince George's destiny has been tied to those "Christmas trees." The first sawmill, built in South Fort George in 1909, was followed by hundreds.

The arrival of pulp mills in the 1960s caused a dramatic change. For the wood chips to manufacture pulp, sawmills employed more sophisticated equipment. Close utilization and a demand for specialized lumber by foreign markets brought about a consolidation of operations.

From a lonely outpost, established in 1806 by Simon Fraser on the banks of the river that bears his name, Prince George has grown to become the second-largest city in British Columbia. Little could Fraser have imagined that an important pulp and lumber, transportation, and manufacturing centre would stand on the site of his modest Fort George.

A century later a rumor that Fort George would become a divisional point on the Grand Trunk Pacific Railway sparked a flurry of activity that saw the population swell and land prices soar. It took a special kind of entrepreneur to leave more settled areas to venture into the remote central interior of the province to encourage commerce and create a city.

Prince George's principal assets have always been people and trees. The growth and progress of the city has been the result of co-operation of civic government, the business community, and its citizens. The organizations whose histories appear in this chapter have chosen to support the Prince George Chamber of Commerce in this important literary and civic project. They clearly represent the spirit of Prince George.

119

PRINCE GEORGE CHAMBER OF COMMERCE

The Prince George Chamber of Commerce marked its 75th year of service to the community in 1986.

Harry G. Perry, the chamber's first elected president, took office in 1915 and served until 1919. He went on to become mayor of the city for three terms—1917, 1918, and 1920; was elected to the provincial legislature representing the Fort George constituency from 1920 to 1928 and again from 1933 to 1946; was speaker of the house from 1933 to 1937; and was Minister of Education from 1941 to 1945.

President for the 1988-1989 term is Judy Jackson, the first woman ever elected to this position. In addition to her long career in local broadcasting, Jackson brings the experience of considerable community involvement to the office. Working with general manager Helen de Groot, the chamber staff, and a 14-member board, Jackson anticipates a busy and productive year.

The Prince George Chamber of Commerce came into being as the Fort George Board of Trade on September 7, 1911. William A. Stillingfleet was sworn in as secretary by D.G.M. Perkins, Justice of the Peace.

Early membership consisted of business people not unlike the members of today. Where yesterday's members were liverymen, horse dealers, and blacksmiths, today's members are bankers, realtors, merchants, manufacturers, printers, lumber operators, restaurant owners, and transportation personnel.

In 1915 the chamber's name was changed to Prince George Board of Trade, and officers were elected for the first time. Early in 1961 the name was again changed, to Prince George Chamber of Commerce.

Records are not available for the years 1937 to 1948, suggesting that during these pre- and postwar years community leaders were addressing themselves to more immediate and pressing problems. The same supposition can be applied to a gap in record keeping from 1961 to 1968, boom years during which the community was caught up in an unprecedented period of growth.

In 1985 the formation of a visitors and convention bureau gave the chamber a clear mandate for business support. Working for You became the slogan for strong, active committees working to make Prince George a better place in which to live and work. A population of nearly 70,000 people is today served by a 350-member chamber.

The board of trade and, more recently, the chamber of commerce have been involved in all major issues and events from the arrival of railroads and prohibition, to extending highways and establishing air service and pulp mills. Dedicated members of the business community have, and are today, working to attract people and investment to the city and area.

General manager Helen de Groot observes, "We are moving into the future with fellow organizations such as the Prince George Region Development Corporation. Sometimes, in looking ahead, it's a good idea to look back to see how far we've come. As sponsor of *The Illustrated History of Prince George,* we're proud to be a part of documenting our colorful past and join in commending the community-minded businesses included in the Partners in Progress chapter, and the professional and dedicated work of authors Bev Christensen and Maureen Keibel."

Left: Harry G. Perry served from 1914 to 1919 as the first elected president of the Fort George Board of Trade, predecessor of the Prince George Chamber of Commerce.

Judy Jackson (center), serving the 1988-1989 term, is the first woman ever elected president of the chamber. The organization's general manager is Helen de Groot (right).

HOWAT INSURANCE BROKERS INC.

Bob Howat came to Prince George with the intention of staying three years—that was 20 years ago.

In 1968 Howat's employer, Commercial Union Insurance, recognizing his close ties with industry, transferred him to the booming central interior city. A year with the Insurance Corporation of British Columbia (ICBC) served to enhance his automobile insurance experience. In 1975 Howat entered into a partnership with local insurance agent Clyde Porter, creating Porter & Howat Insurance.

At that time the business was a small personal-lines office representing only 10 insurance companies. Today this representation has increased to the point where the services of almost every major company is offered, with access to both domestic and international markets.

Founded in 1969 by the late Clyde Porter, the firm, originally known as Porter & Johnston, was located at 817 Victoria Street and employed a staff of five, compared with the present 18. Many long-term employees have served to offer continuity throughout the many changes in the industry and within the agency itself.

In 1977 the growing firm demanded larger premises, and the present building at 901 Victoria Street was constructed to accommodate increased staff and services.

Clyde Porter's untimely death in 1983 saw the firm experience major readjustments while continuing to successfully serve commercial and domestic clients. In July of that year the agency became Howat Insurance Brokers Inc.

Under Bob Howat's astute guidance the firm has grown to offer, in addition to general insurance, all lines of insurance and brokerage services. Aware of the trends in the industry, Howat saw a need for a more comprehensive service—one that encompassed more than insurance. What evolved was a financial service that offers, in addition to insurance brokerage, professional investment guidance.

Howat Insurance is well equipped to offer a financial planning service, including mutual funds and RRSPs. Other financial services are being developed to assist clients in today's changing money market. To keep abreast of the rapid changes brought about by demands from society, business, and industry, Howat Insurance employees are constantly adding to their knowledge of insurance and financial planning.

In addition, the tradition of professionalism established by founder Clyde Porter is maintained throughout the company. Client needs and best interests are always the main considerations. Howat observes, "The level of professionalism offered by our brokerage is most certainly equal to, and in some cases exceeds, that offered anywhere in the province."

Despite the expansion of services, Howat Insurance has managed to preserve its original goal of providing personalized service while at the same time

Robert A. Howat, president.

expanding services and incorporating modern innovations such as computerization.

It comes as no surprise that a large percentage of Howat Insurance Brokers Inc.'s clientele has been doing business with the firm since 1969. Recently introduced brokerage and financial planning services have expanded the client base to include larger and more complex accounts.

Howat Insurance Brokers Inc. has played an important role in the history of Prince George and is destined to be an essential part of its future growth.

B.C. FOREST SERVICE
PRINCE GEORGE FOREST REGION

The Prince George Forest Region lies in the northwest quadrant of British Columbia. It is larger than the United Kingdom and occupies more than one-quarter of the province. Forty-two percent (58.5 million acres) of British Columbia's forest land lies with the Prince George Forest Region.

On April 1, 1913, the first division of the province into forest districts came into effect, and the first forest service office was opened in Prince George under the direction of district forester G.D. McKay.

The following year the Prince George Forest District executed its first timber sale, and British Columbia led in lumber production that year with 1,151,903 board feet, just slightly ahead of Quebec, which produced 1,118,298 board feet. The total revenue received from forest sources in 1913 was $2,999,328 as compared to $210.26 million in 1986.

The education of the public in regard to the value of the forest resources was a prime concern in 1915, even as it is today. New posters were put up each year along roads and trails, and around watering places and camp grounds. Motion picture theatres throughout the province showed slides, furnished by the Forest Service, bearing warnings about carelessness with fire in the woods. The total number of forest fires recorded in 1913 was 578. The 1985/1986 fire season saw a total of 3,603 fires. Then, as now, the majority of the fires were caused by campers and travellers.

In 1927, the first year detailed records were kept, the staff of the Fort George District office numbered 15 members with a total salary list of $26,000 per year. Supervisors were not considered necessary. In 1988 the regular staff in the Prince George Regional Forest Service totalled 92, of whom approximately 20 were supervisors.

The Aleza Lake Experiment Station was created in 1924 and research was started to determine the source of seed from which reproduction could be expected. It was noted with concern that the exhaustion of the virgin stands would only be a question of time, due to the increasing demands of the lumber market. Good silviculture practices became an important issue, and planting studies were undertaken.

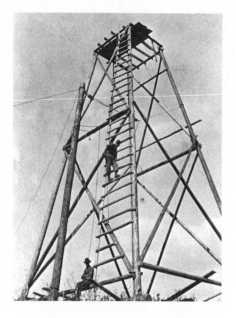

Construction of British Columbia Forest Service lookout tower at Isle Pierre, 1927.

Many chief foresters spent time in the Prince George Forest District, including Mickey Pogue, Lorne Swannel (after whom the mountain range was named), Bill Young, and John Cuthbert, present chief forester.

Ray Williston, Ministry of Lands and Forests from 1956 to 1972, is credited with being the most important individual in the history of forest industry in northern British Columbia. Through introduction of pulp-harvesting licences and close utilization, Williston was responsible for the establishment of pulp mills that dramatically changed the industry and populated the North.

Today the Prince George Forest Region thrives under the direction of regional manager Fred Baxter. The hard work of dedicated foresters and technicians throughout the years has helped Prince George to become The White Spruce Capital of the World.

District Forester's headquarters at Tete Jaune, 1913.

B.C. LANDS

Since the 1858 Cariboo gold rush, miners, loggers, and homesteaders have been buying and leasing crown lands in the Prince George area.

Originally, the field inspections and reports were submitted to Victoria by the local forest rangers. However, in the post-World War II boom, the demand for crown land exploded. As a result, the Department of Lands and Forests hired a small team of university-trained land inspectors for the province and set up a one-man office in Prince George on June 1, 1947.

Tom Hyslop, B.C. Lands' first land inspector, was hired at a salary of $185 per month. Given an upstairs office at Third and Brunswick, a part-time stenographer, and a 1948 sedan, his inspection area stretched from McLeese Lake to Burns Lake and included the Vale-mount area.

A large part of the early field travel was done by horseback and later by riding the C.N.R. freight trains to Longworth, Penny, Dome Creek, and McBride. The department also stored a jeep in McBride to allow the field staff to drive to Valemount and Alberta.

In 1950 the Lands Branch could have sold a Prince George town lot for $100. But in the summer of 1955 the city experienced a land boom caused by the John Hart Highway and the completion of the extension of the Pacific and Great Eastern Rail Line from Quesnel. Industrial land prices in Prince George soared and soon exceeded those of Vancouver and Edmonton. As a result of this activity, the land office expanded to a two-man team in 1958.

Today inspection work is conducted by helicopter, pickup truck, river boat, and even the occasional horseback trip. The Prince George Lands Office has expanded to 23 full-time staff members, including five land inspectors. All leases and licences are now issued locally, using a sophisticated province-wide computer network. The current portfolio of more than 2,500 leases includes the new P.G. Automobile Racing Association (P.G.A.R.A) track, the Hickory Wing Ski Club House on Otway Road, Mr. Pee Gee on Highway 16, Forests for the World on Cranbrook Hill, and the Sears Auto Centre.

Having served the Prince George area for 41 years, B.C. Lands anticipates meeting the future needs of the community.

A 1948 Ford equipped with high boy wheels (to better traverse rough roads) is shown on Blue River Road in 1948.

B.C. TELEPHONE COMPANY

"Hello, Central?"

In the early 1900s making a telephone call involved contacting the operator, who was always referred to as "Central."

Christine M. Taylor, writing in the *Vancouver Province* on September 9, 1944, told readers: "The telephone service of the old days was indeed an example of what the public can expect from a well-blended mixture of sympathy and curiosity. Central was a local girl, and she always knew where everyone was; she had the advantage of being placed high up in a central building, and what she couldn't see she could hear; she could tell you if

formed by the British Columbia Telephone Company to enter the radio-telephone field.

Radio-telephone offered the only practical method of servicing isolated areas. In anticipation of the extended service, a new building on Fourth Avenue was opened December 9, 1930. Radio-telephone service was restricted to daylight hours—9 a.m. to 6 p.m.

On November 3, 1932, Prince George was able to talk to the outside world for the first time.

February 1951 saw a new business office opened at 433 George Street, and a year later a growing number of logging and sawmill oper-

came headquarters for the Northern Division and district headquarters for Prince George.

Work continued on construction of microwave systems to connect the central interior with the Trans-Canada Microwave System. Live network television by the Canadian Broadcasting System reached Prince George on March 1, 1965, through B.C. Tel's microwave system.

Technological upgrading is ongoing at B.C. Tel. In 1988 construction began on the link-up with Telecom Canada's coast-to-coast Lightguide Transmission System project, which has a completion

New TSPS (Traffic Service Position Systems) used today for operator-handled long-distance calls. Courtesy, British Columbia Telephone Company

Mrs. E. Barber of the recently closed Dawson Creek office completes a long-distance call on a 31 board. Courtesy, British Columbia Telephone Company

the doctor had come back from the hospital, and if your husband's car was outside the store or over at the fire station."

The Fort George and Alberta Telephone & Electric Company Limited, incorporated December 30, 1909, to service the Fort George area, went into voluntary liquidation in 1929. The plant was purchased by the North West Telephone Company, a venture

ations in the area received service, with the installation of a medium-frequency radio-telephone system.

A further step in providing sophisticated equipment was taken in 1954, when a new, 10-relay-station radio chain was opened to provide very-high-frequency circuits between Vancouver and Prince George. A microwave radio-telephone system through the Cariboo, providing additional long-distance circuits from Vancouver to Prince George, was completed by 1959.

The B.C. Telephone Company officially took over North West Telephone in 1961. Prince George be-

target of 1990. Incorporation of fibre-optics development and laser technology will provide virtually noise-free transmission.

Prince George residents made 5,933,829 direct-distance-dialing calls in 1987. While technology may have replaced calling "Central," B.C. Telephone Company customers still find an attentive ear and willing assistance when they dial the operator.

NORTHLAND PLYMOUTH CHRYSLER LTD.

The Prince George area had been without a Chrysler dealership for more than two years when Northland Plymouth Chrysler Ltd. opened its doors in June 1984. Founding partners Glen Wicklund, Henry Reimer, and Gary Hehn believed opportunity existed in the central interior city, even though the economy, emerging from a recession, was not buoyant at the time.

The decision to locate downtown saw them settle on the site of a former automobile dealership at Third Avenue and Victoria Street. Leaning heavily on the talents of Hehn, a building contractor by trade, the facility was restored, adding considerably to the appearance and stability of the area.

Wicklund had become involved with Chrysler products as an apprentice at Begg Motors in Vancouver in 1958, Reimer worked for a Chrysler dealer in Winnipeg in 1962 and worked his way west. Continuing their association with Chrysler in the service area, the two met in 1969, kept in touch, and in the early 1980s decided to pool their resources and experience in forming their own Chrysler dealership. (Hehn has returned to the construction industry.)

A shared commitment to quality and customer service echoed Chrysler president Lee Iacocca's pledge to the motoring public when he restructured that corporation in 1981. Consumer acceptance of the K cars and other retooled Chrysler products helped to establish the dealership on a firm footing.

Wicklund and Reimer share a simple philosophy that involves putting the customer first regardless of cost or circumstances. They believe the excellent product, qualified staff, downtown location, extended hours, and commitment to quality ensure customer satisfaction. "Service," says Wicklund, "is

Glen Wicklund (right) and partner Henry Reimer with Chrysler Service Excellence awards in the background. Courtesy, **The Prince George Citizen**

the foundation of our business. Our philosophy is based on providing customer satisfaction at all times. Northland delivers vehicles as far away as Burns Lake, Smithers, and even Terrace."

"It's part of the service," adds Reimer. "When you sell a vehicle you should be there to make the presentation and thank the customer. Should there be a problem, we're close at hand and ready to be of service."

Proof of Northland's commitment to service hangs on the wall in Wicklund's office. Out of 530 dealerships Northland has for two consecutive years been among the 26 chosen for Chrysler Service Excellence awards.

Starting with a staff of five, the fledgling dealership added 20 more employees during the first year and now boasts a total of 50. In addition to their individual automotive expertise, each employee has successfully completed the Super Host Program, a specially designed course dealing with serving the public. With an eye toward

the future, Northland Plymouth Chrysler is finalizing plans for a new dealership on three acres in downtown Prince George.

Community involvement is another commitment Wicklund and Reimer have honored since the beginning. Both are enthusiastic Prince George supporters, tirelessly promoting shopping at home. When need is made known, Northland Chrysler is quick to respond, with a car for a parade, transporting visiting dignitaries, or other special occasions. The College of New Caledonia Automotive Apprenticeship Program receives support through two Auto Trade bursaries. Many community events depend on business sponsorship, and Northland Plymouth Chrysler Ltd. is happy to participate, not only in Prince George, but also in Mackenzie, Vanderhoof, McBride, and other neighboring communities.

CROSSROADS CONSTRUCTION

John Row's competitors want to know what kind of coffee he buys. Crossroads Construction, Row's firm, is one of the most successful in Prince George. He says it is because he puts the coffee on early in the morning.

"I try to be in my office no later than seven o'clock in the morning," explains Row with a smile. "The men know if they arrive at a quarter after seven, they can have a cup of coffee. And believe it or not, I get three quarters of an hour of advice and assistance from them. It is a great time for sharing ideas and concerns. And it doesn't cost me a cent."

Row, named by the Federal Business Development Bank/Chamber of Commerce as Businessman of the Year in 1986, is a good example of someone "managing for success." His reference to the coffee pot and how it has been instrumental in Crossroads' growth is actually a reference to people. The key to Row's success is people and how he deals with them.

Werner Pietrek has been with Crossroads for 25 years, several others almost that long—the average length of employment being 8.5 years. People and how they feel about a company result in the kind of professionalism associated with Crossroads.

Row's administrative team consists of supervisor and contracts manager Dennis Schwab, estimator Nino Maletta, and office manager Elaine Scott. An enthusiastic supporter of the apprenticeship and College of New Caledonia construction technology programs, Row points out that some apprentices have moved up to fill the positions of foreman, and two of his administration people are graduates of the construction technology program.

Row operates a union shop and this, he believes, has been the reason the firm has been able to get work with many of its long-term customers, such as Northwood Pulp & Timber, Prince George Pulp & Paper Mill, B.C. Telephone Company, Lakeland Mills Ltd., B.C. Forest Service, Ministry of Transportation & Highways, and Quintette Coal. "These people have continued to give us work over the years when the years were tough. If it wasn't for the customers we have, we wouldn't have survived. They've been excellent, and we intend to look after them."

Crossroads Construction, originally Cloverdale Construction North, was established in Prince George by Stan Stagg in 1962. Stagg, who served as alderman of the City of Prince George from 1965 to 1967 when Garvin Dezell was mayor, opened the first office at 1797 Lyon Street. Joining Crossroads in 1964, Row bought an interest in the company a year later and in 1972 acquired 100 percent of the shares to become president.

Originally a general contracting firm, Crossroads began diversifying into other areas, including heavy civil construction with an emphasis on bridges, roads, and related work for the forest industry. Other areas are construction and project management, commercial construction, design development for industrial construction, and underground installations.

Completed Crossroads projects in and around the city include the Phoenix and Victoria Medical buildings, the Royal Bank and Imperial Bank of Commerce on Third Avenue, the rebuilt intersection at the junction of highways 97 and 16, an addition to the Prince George Regional Hospital, and several schools—Blackburn, Peden Hill, Harwin, and Seymour.

Above: John Row, named Businessman of the Year by the Federal Business Development Bank/Chamber, uses a pot of coffee as an effective management tool. Photo by Brock Gable

Bottom: British Columbia Telephone, one of Crossroads' long-term customers, commissioned the firm to build its Telephone Control Building at Tambler Ridge.

Crossroads' client list reads like the who's who of industry and includes such names as Northwood Pulp & Timber, B.C. Forest Products, Quintette Coal, Finlay Forest Products, B.C. Telephone, Lakeland Mills, Canfor, Dominion Bridge, the City of Prince George. The list keeps growing.

Some of Crossroads Construction's projects have included Binwall installation on the Crooked River Bridge, Hart Highway, in 1985 (left), and the 1988 construction of Zeidler Forest Product's bridge over the Fraser River, near McBride (right).

As well as projects in Prince George and the surrounding area, Crossroads has done work in Prince Rupert, the Okanagan, Dawson Creek, Fort St. John, Tumbler Ridge, and Grimshaw, Alberta.

Row believes his company is capable of handling unique jobs—those that require the firm's special kind of problem-solving ability. His versatile staff is able to be both innovative and practical in its approach to individual situations.

"It's tougher to be in business today," says Row. "You have to work harder, be more aware, and be aware of the competition. In the 1960s there might be four bidders on a job, none from out of town. Now there are more local bidders and as many as four from out of town."

The success of this approach is apparent in Crossroads' annual volume, which is in excess of $5 million with approximately 250 to 300 projects contributing to this figure.

The firm has twice received The Ross Award, given annually by architect Stuart Ross to a firm exhibiting high standards of business ethics.

Row does not restrict his activities to the drawing board or the construction site. He has served on most of the Prince George Construction Association committees and board of directors, and has twice served a president of that organization. Community involvement also includes membership in the chamber of commerce, Rotary, and Shrine clubs.

Adept at time management, Row arranges to spend as much time as possible with his wife, Mary; his son, Graham (who works with him); his two daughters, Karen and Cheryl; and three grandchildren, all in Prince George.

A successful businessman, Row has faith in the future of Prince George and Crossroads Construction. His success can, in many ways, be attributed to his uncomplicated approach to life and doing business.

Tom Peters, in his best-selling management book for the 1980s, *In Search of Excellence,* recommends, "Management by Wandering Around" and "Short Lines of Communication Between Top Management and the Staff." At Crossroads Construction, talking to the boss is as simple as talking to the guy who makes the coffee.

One of Crossroads' more unusual projects was the water slide at the Four Seasons Pool Complex in Prince George.

REED STENHOUSE LTD.

The history of Reed Stenhouse Ltd., one of the largest retail brokerage operations with more than 250 offices and 17,000 employees, dates back to 1850. Today the Prince George office takes pride in offering the same personal service as its predecessor company, Carmichael & Luttrell Agencies Ltd. did.

In 1953 T.S. "Tommy" Carmichael resigned his position as principal of King George V Elementary School after 23 years as an educator, and entered the business world. In buying out W.S. Russell Real Estate he acquired a partner in Ken Luttrell, who had recently resigned as provincial deputy assessor in Prince George to pursue a career in real estate and insurance. Carmichael & Luttrell started with a staff of six.

Tommy Carmichael is well remembered for his community involvement, having spent six years on the city council, serving as president of the Cariboo Real Estate Board, and as a member of the Rotary Club and Elk's Lodge. He died in 1986.

Ken Luttrell, a six-year veteran with the Seaforth Highlanders, also served as president of the Cariboo Real Estate Board, as a member of the Kiwanis Club, and as a director of the Senior Citizens' Home Society. He was also one of the few notary publics in the city. Luttrell died in 1984.

The successful partnership in real estate and insurance continued until 1959, when Carmichael sold his interest in the company to Gordon and Evelyn Baillie. At that time Luttrell became president, a title he held until his retirement.

Carmichael & Luttrell purchased L.T. Kenney's office at Fourth Avenue and George Street. A short while later the company, using the federal government Do-it-Now Winter Works Program, constructed a new building (now The Pastry Chef) at 380 George Street.

As one of the oldest real estate and insurance offices in the city, Carmichael & Luttrell continued to serve Prince George and vicinity until 1971. At that time the insurance division was amalgamated with the British Columbia insurance operations of Armstrong & Taylor Limited. Sigmund Bekken, who had served as insurance manager for Carmichael & Luttrell, was appointed se-

Jacques Fournier, AIIC.

nior representative. Jacob Esau represented the firm in Mackenzie, Harvey Milne in Vanderhoof. The real estate division became known as Spruce City Realty.

Meanwhile, Stenhouse Holdings Limited, a company well established throughout the world except for North America, merged with Reed Shaw Osler, a Canadian firm with no international facilities. Each wanted access to the U.S. market. The merger achieved these goals through the U.S. firm of Reed Shaw Stenhouse, Inc. Ultimately the company became Reed Stenhouse Ltd., the world's largest retail brokerage operation. Further mergers resulted in the firm becoming Reed Shaw Stenhouse, Inc., and ultimately Reed Stenhouse Ltd.

In 1971 Armstrong & Taylor, formerly Carmichael & Luttrell, merged with Reed Shaw Osler Ltd. Bekken was succeeded by David Naismith in 1973, and Alan Stead became branch manager nine years later.

Today, under the direction of Jacques Fournier, who in 1988 became vice-president in charge of the Prince George office, Reed Stenhouse Ltd. serves a wide client base and anticipates a long and prosperous association with the area.

Ken Luttrell, R.I. (B.C.), 1915-1984.

T.S. Carmichael, 1899-1986.

THE PAS LUMBER COMPANY

In its 34-year history in Prince George, The Pas Lumber Company has gone from whipsaws to lasers. Today it is one of the most modern mills in North America, utilizing a sophisticated network of computer and laser equipment, and it has come a long way since "the sawdust twins," Dave and Charlie, started the Winton Lumber Company in Wausau, Wisconsin, in 1889.

Late in 1987, just short of the Winton's marking 100 years as a continuously run family operation, The Pas Lumber Company was purchased by local lumbermen Bob Stewart, Ivan Andersen, and George Killy.

The Winton's first move into the Canadian lumber industry was in 1905. Following acquisition of several operations in Saskatchewan, The Pas Lumber Company Ltd. at The Pas, Manitoba, was purchased in 1918.

The family's perseverance and commitment to the lumber business have been tested on a number of occasions. There were two false starts in British Columbia. The Eagle Lake sawmill, built at Giscome in 1922, was sold during the Depression. A second unsuccessful attempt at establishing an operation in British Columbia was made in Kamloops in the 1940s. It was in 1955 that The Pas Lumber Company bought the old Hales-Ross planer mill on River Road in Prince George, the site of the existing mill.

A sawmill, built at Fish Hook Lake, near the Parsnip River, in 1956 and destroyed by fire three years later, was replaced by a new mill at Anzac in 1961. There followed a series of acquisitions, beginning with the purchase of the Stevens and Rahn sawmill at Kerry Lake in 1963, the Merton Lake sawmill in 1967, and Park Brothers' Summit Lake operation in 1969.

Construction of a two-line mill at mile 42 on the Hart Highway near Bear Lake (today known as the Hart Sawmill Division) in 1972 served to consolidate the three smaller mills. A third side was added in 1975 to accommodate timber from the Anzac Mill when the isolated location forced shutdown of that operation.

Lumber from the Hart Sawmill Division, as was the lumber from the smaller mills earlier, is transported to Prince George where it is stored, dried, dressed, and shipped from the planer mill on River Road.

In 1979 The Pas Lumber Company built what is generally recognized as the most modern structural grade finger-jointed long-length dimension mill in North America at a cost of $2.5 million.

Always known as "a good place to work,"—numerous families have had two or three generations employed at the same time—The Pas has demonstrated its commitment to people in many ways. Christmas turkeys for employees is a tradition that is continued today. Longtime employees recall the luxury of heated outhouses in the remote camps, a feature unique to The Pas Lumber Company.

The Pas' corporate commitment extends to many areas in the community. A recent contribution of $150,000 toward the development of the riverfront park and trail system has made possible an all-season recreation facility within the city.

The Pas Lumber Company is a colorful part of Prince George's heritage and its future.

The Hales-Ross planer mill on River Road in Prince George, pictured here in 1954, was purchased by The Pas Lumber Company in 1955 and serves as the site of the firm's existing planer operation.

HOLIDAY INN-PRINCE GEORGE

Many important people have enjoyed the hospitality of the Holiday Inn-Prince George since it opened in the Plaza 400 on October 30, 1981. Prime Minister Brian Mulroney and Rick Hansen stayed there.

The Plaza 400 complex, competed in 1979, had a tremendous impact on George Street in particular and downtown Prince George in general. Covering an entire block, the complex houses, in addition to the Holiday Inn, provincial government offices, a Famous Players Twin theatre, and several retail outlets.

The first innkeeper at the six-

were borrowed from the hotel to seat the royal visitors during their appearance in Prince George.

In addition to its attractively appointed, soundproof guest rooms, the hotel offers two deluxe suites, the Tabor and Purden, each complete with living room, guest powder room, large bedroom with panoramic view, and double-size Jacuzzi bath. The Cottonwood, Engleman, Tamarack, and Lodgepole meeting rooms offer state-of-the-art audiovisual equipment. Guests are invited to relax in the leisure area on the third floor, where a swimming pool, sauna, and whirlpool await the weary traveller.

they enjoy offering this special kind of hospitality to visitors and local residents alike. The success of their endeavors is reflected in the two superior awards, earned in both 1986 and 1987. Of the 1,800 Holiday Inns, only 12 have received this award for two consecutive years.

In 1962 David Rubinoff persuaded Kemmons Wilson of Memphis, Tennessee, founder of Holiday Inns Incorporated of America, to grant him a foreign franchise. Rubinoff's first Holiday Inn was opened in London, Ontario, in June 1962. Since that time the company has grown to be the largest Ca-

storey, 139-room Holiday Inn was Gerhard Felgenhauer, who had as his assistant manager Graham Holmes, now hotel manager. Holmes, a fervent royalist, was manager in May 1986 when Prince Charles and Princess Diana came to town to open The B.C. Festival of the Arts. Their itinerary allowed for the Royal Couple to spend "rest time" at the Holiday Inn. The hotel staff engaged in a frenzy of activity in preparation for the famous guests, but at the last minute, plans were changed, and the Royals were whisked off to Vancouver and Expo '86 duties. The story has a humorous ending though—two upholstered chairs

Left: Holiday Inn-Prince George.

Right: The well-appointed lobby offers easy access to Traders' Restaurant, Coach's Corner Pub, and Den Lounge.

The 20,000-square-foot main floor houses, in addition to the spacious lobby, the attractively appointed Cranbrook Ballroom; Traders Restaurant; The Den Lounge; the Coach's Corner, a sports-oriented pub; Wagers Casino, open seven days a week; Sheffield and Son's Gift Shop; and Joyceline's Beauty Salon.

The staff of 120 professionals takes pride in the reputation enjoyed by Holiday Inns worldwide;

nadian hotelier in the world, with operations in many parts of the western world.

Recently the company name changed from Commonwealth Holiday Inns of Canada Limited to Commonwealth Hospitality Ltd.—a name that indicates a new direction. Diversification includes Briarwood Inns, developed for the value-conscious small business and family travel market, with the first Briarwood opened recently in London, Ontario.

The Holiday Inn-Prince George is proudly maintaining the established tradition of outstanding hospitality—guests can be sure of receiving a royal welcome.

DELOITTE HASKINS & SELLS

Deloitte Haskins & Sells has, since 1924, merged with more than 60 other accounting firms, most recently with Samson, Belair. It has emerged as one of the top three chartered accountancy firms in Canada and a major partner in Deloitte Haskins & Sells International, with affiliated firms in more than 60 countries worldwide.

DH&S is an independent Canadian firm that evolved from an office established in Montreal in 1912, under the name Deloitte, Plender, Griffiths & Co. It was first established as an autonomous Canadian partnership in 1954, upon merger with the Winnipeg-based firm of Miller, McDonald & Co. The firm marked its 75th anniversary in 1986.

With representation in Prince George since 1955, DH&S has had a colorful history in the central interior of British Columbia. In 1923 Herbert J. Paisley & Co. was servicing clients in the Prince George area. This practice continued until 1951, when W.R. "Bill" Hollingshead opened an office in the Masonic Hall building on Fourth Avenue in Prince George for Herbert J. Paisley and one in Quesnel a year later. The firm became Paisley, Wallace & Co., and merged with Deloitte, Plender, Haskins & Sells three years later, giving that firm its first Prince George representation.

In 1959 the Quesnel practice was sold to Douglas Johnston, who merged it with Fry, Rigsby & Co. to form Rigsby, Johnston & Co. This firm established a Prince George office that merged with DH&S 10 years later, bringing in partners L.A. Jewitt, R.W. Lungren, and J.W. Watson and office secretary Joyce Davidson. The original managing partner was Bill Hollingshead, until illness forced him to retire in 1969, when Paul Ken-

way took his place. Kenway's retirement saw Ken Little become managing partner until his transfer to the Regina office.

At this time Lou Jewitt became managing partner until the merger with Winspear, Higgins, Stevenson & Co. in 1980. Both predecessor firms had practised in Prince George for some time. Mike McGillivray opened the Winspear office in 1964, arriving from Dawson Creek when a local practice was acquired from Leo Crowe, a DH&S alumnus. Many of the clients at that time were in the Vanderhoof area, 60 miles west, and a number of these continue to be clients today.

At the time of the merger McGillivray assumed the role of managing partner. This merger produced an office of approximately 65 people with partners McGillivray, Jewitt, Charles Buchan, Brent Campbell, Robert McFarlane, George Otterbein (now in Regina), Victor Schwab, Bud Sweany (now involved in his own practice), and Jim Watson, who has since joined a local firm. John Paterson was admitted as a partner in 1982.

The firm located in its current premises on the fifth floor of the Canada Permanent Tower in 1977 (the Canada Trust Tower).

Partners in Deloitte Haskins & Sells, Prince George, include (top row, from left) Ralph Hagen, Charles Buchan, Brent Campbell, and Victor Schwab. In the bottom row (from left) are Robert McFarlane, Louis Jewitt, managing partner Michael McGillivray, and John Paterson.

In 1985 McGillivray was seconded to the British Columbia Development Corporation as acting chief executive officer, and Lou Jewitt assumed the position of managing partner with DH&S. When McGillivray's secondment appeared to be more of a permanent situation, Jewitt was appointed managing partner of the Prince George office.

DH&S serves an area with a radius of approximately 150 miles; however, the firm has clients in Smithers (450 miles west), Kelowna, Vancouver, and Victoria, British Columbia, and provides service to ex-Winspear offices in Dawson Creek and Fort St. John, with a complement of 51 full-time and four part-time personnel.

Deloitte Haskins & Sells is proud to serve Prince George, with a client base that includes many local independent sawmills, related industries, professional practices, and small businesses.

LAKELAND MILLS LTD.

Throughout the year businessmen from Tokyo or London or Atlanta often may be seen driving down River Road in Prince George. They are on their way to Lakeland Mills, to see the source of their supplies of softwood lumber.

Lakeland's distinctive blue-end construction studs are the premium choice of builders on four continents. In factories Lakeland is known as the producer of wood components piece workers never reject. A recognized mark of quality throughout the United States, the United Kingdom, Europe, Asia, the Middle East, and the Caribbean is the Lakeland symbol: an L shape cut from a conifer and formed by scale representations of two- by three-foot, two- by four-foot, and two- by six-foot studs.

The roots of Lakeland Mills are in the richest softwood forests of North America. Spruce, pine, and fir grow slowly in a harsh climate similar to Scandinavia's. The long growing season produces tightly ringed timber of unusually high quality—fine white wood with small knots.

Lakeland Mills has harvested this tall tree country for more

than a quarter-century. Since the firm was founded in 1963, it has been owned and operated by Prince George lumbermen—men for whom forestry is family tradition. The owners of Lakeland Mills today are Ivan Andersen, George Killy, and Bob Stewart.

In 1979 Lakeland Mills began to introduce technological innovations to the production of lumber. The company installed electronic equipment that would dramatically increase efficiency and produc-

tivity and improve quality control. Soon the computer became as common as the saw. Laser beam scanners were employed to analyze logs and determine their most profitable use. Recovery rates (the amount of marketable lumber extracted from raw logs) rose to levels that would have astonished lumbermen of earlier eras. In 1984 Lakeland Mills received the Canada Award for excellence in recognition of "labor-management cooperation and implementation of technological change."

The most recent implementation of technological change at Lakeland was the development and construction of a highly sophisticated planer mill. When this 68,000-square-foot facility began operation in the summer of 1988, it introduced equipment and systems new to North America. This advanced facility is capable of producing precision-cut

Above: Computerized sawing solutions result in exceptional accuracy and consistency. Lakeland Mills won the Canada Award for excellence in labor-management co-operation toward technological change.

Left: The richest softwood forests in North America produce the spruce, pine, and fir timber delivered to Lakeland's log deck.

pieces in lengths from two to eight feet.

Many of the mill's products are unique, created specifically to customer request. George Killy says, "We're delighted to have the market look to us for custom design and to have customers come here to take part in the production process." Some buyers travel from the other side of the Pacific Rim to watch the first run of products they have commissioned.

The market looks to Lakeland Mills not only for design and production capabilities, but also for a long-term supply of quality white softwood lumber. Lakeland currently produces more than 125 million board feet per year. To transport that extraordinary output, a Canadian National Railways spur line runs through the planer mill.

That indoor rail line and a sheltered loading platform for giant trucks mean that lumber produced by Lakeland is protected from weather damage from the time the bark-covered logs arrive at the mill until the finished lumber is delivered to the customer. Lumber to be shipped by freighter is packed in containers. Not a drop of rain, a speck of mud, or a ray of sunshine touches the lumber between Prince George and Tokyo.

To ensure that its supply of superior softwood continues, Lakeland Mills conducts its own reforestation program. A research project for the rehabilitation of a prime growing cut was developed by the company's forestry and engineering department in conjunction with the British

Precision-cut lumber in two- to eight-foot lengths is produced by Lakeland's planer mill. The mill's sophisticated technology is commissioned for many custom design projects.

Columbia Forest Service. The project was established on 137 hectares in an area called Foreman Flats. The result was a tree farm for Lakeland, now managed by its woods department, and an experimental pilot project for the B.C. Forest Service. Similar programs are now being applied in other regions of the province.

That means that for as far into the future as anyone can see, ea-

Lumber is loaded onto boxcars on the CNR spur line that runs through the planer mill. Lakeland Mills' lumber is completely sheltered from the time the logs arrive at the mill until the finished product reaches the customer.

gles will nest in the tall timber of Prince George while boxcars, flatbed trucks, and ocean freighters carry lumber with the Lakeland Mills stamp to builders worldwide.

PRINCE GEORGE WOOD PRESERVING LTD.

Prince George Wood Preserving Ltd., on Willow Cale Road, started out as a retirement hobby for its president and has grown into a multimillion-dollar operation with markets worldwide.

Incorporated on April 1, 1977, by president Gordon Swanky, managing director Don Flynn, and partner Dean Shaw, the plant was operational in March 1978. When Shaw withdrew from the partnership in 1979, Wayne Kidd and Gerry Dell became shareholders.

A research and development program on lodgepole pine resulted in the plant being certified by the Ca-

Gordon Erik Swanky (1927-1987) incorporated Prince George Wood Preserving Ltd. in 1977. His career in lumber began with his father's Canyon Tie and Timber Sawmill.

nadian Standards Association for treating lodgepole pine lumber and fir plywood. Prior to this research it was generally believed impossible to treat interior species to an acceptable standard. The cellular structure of spruce will not accept the chemicals that fir will, to make it almost impervious to decay. Preserved wood basements, with the energy-saving feature of being warmer than concrete, quickly became popular.

During the bullish lumber markets of 1978 and 1979, when interior mills were producing spruce dimension lumber, it was difficult to obtain pine lumber. This shortage led to the construction of a sawmill and planermill.

At this time a devastating spruce beetle epidemic broke out in the Prince George East Forest District. The British Columbia Forest Service and the industry concentrated on harvesting the beetle-infested timber. Prince George Wood Preserving, under the Ministry of Forests' Small Business Enterprise Program, applied for registration under category 2 and successfully bid on its first Crown Timber Sale in January 1981. When category 2 allotment was increased, the firm responded with a sawmill expansion.

The United Kingdom's concern that wood imported from British Columbia might result in the spread of the spruce beetle there resulted in a policy that lumber must be bark free and produced from debarked logs. To remain competitive, barking and chipping equipment was installed.

The upgrading was carried out under the direction of veteran lumbermen Gordon Swanky and Don Flynn—both members of the six-partner consortium that established North Central Plywood, sold to Northwood Pulp & Timber in 1980.

The late Gordon Swanky's lumber experience dates back to involvement in his father's Canyon Tie and Timber Sawmill in the Chief Lake Area, later renamed Hixon Logging. Born in Edmonton, he moved to Prince George as an infant and first lived on a homestead in the Chief Lake area, later attending Baron Byng High School. He enjoyed hockey, both as a participant and as a supporter. He was admired and respected throughout

the industry and his community.

His friend and partner, the late Don Flynn, was born in South Fort George and also attended the old Baron Byng High School. His lumber career began as a sawyer and included 13 years with British Columbia Forest Service, both in silviculture and as a ranger. A partnership in contract logging with his brother Gerald and in North Central Plywood preceded his involvement in founding Prince George Wood Preserving. Well respected in the industry, he was prominent in community activities.

Prince George Wood Preserv-

Donald Murray Flynn (1930-1985) served with the British Columbia Forest Service and did contract logging before co-founding Prince George Wood Preserving Ltd.

ing Ltd., recently purchased by Chris and Paul Winther and Vivian Shaw, has 125 employees and, through its association with Noranda Sales, ships dimensional products to the United Kingdom, Ireland, Scotland, Australia, Holland, Japan, Algeria, and the Middle East, in addition to supplying the domestic market. With Rustad Bros. Co. Ltd. it will undertake the reconstruction and operation of the British Columbia Railway's Takla Extension.

INLAND NATURAL GAS CO. LTD.

An Inland Natural Gas Ltd. crew laying transmission pipeline in the late 1950s.

Newspaper headlines and political infighting, rumors and delegations to city council all led to the decision to award Inland Natural Gas Co. Ltd. exclusive distribution rights in the area. As a result, Inland came to Prince George and stayed.

That was 30 years ago. Inland Natural Gas Co. Ltd. commenced service to 6,000 customers in 27 communities throughout the interior of British Columbia and Prince George one year later. It was the culmination of five years of intensive planning and organization. Under the direction of late president John A. McMahon, the possibility of natural gas service to the interior of the province became a reality with construction of the Westcoast Transmission Pipeline and Inland Natural Gas Co. Ltd. transmission facilities.

There was no precedent for bringing natural gas to a region such as the British Columbia interior. It was, and still is, one of the largest natural gas distribution areas in North America.

Bob Wiggins, Inland's first Prince George manager, worked

with a staff of 15. The hourly rate of pay at the time was $1.80. Present regional manager John Heaslip, who has been with Inland 25 years, directs 45 employees and all of the firm's operations from Williams Lake to Fort Nelson. Heaslip, who has seen considerable growth and change during his time in Prince George, cites natural gas conversion for vehicles, first adopted by Prince George Taxi, as a recent major innovation.

By the end of the 1950s Inland had grown to 13,000 customers and was gaining a foothold in the residential market with aggressive programs to convert households from coal, wood, and oil to natural gas. At the same time a number of industrial contracts were negotiated in the lumber and mining industries. Secondary manufacturing and commercial establishments were switching to natural gas. Inland and its subsidiaries currently serve 140,000 residential, commercial, and industrial customers in 70 communities.

John A. McMahon, president of Inland Natural Gas from 1952 until his death in 1972, was born in Moyie, British Columbia, and

was heading his own investment company when, in 1949, his brother Frank (who was to become president of Westcoast Transmission Co. Ltd.) interested him in forming an organization to distribute natural gas from the Peace River area to the rest of the province. The pipeline was built and operational within a year. McMahon was the soft-spoken but dynamic force that powered Inland through its first 20 years. His faith in the company he organized and co-founded was as steady as the flame that became its corporate symbol.

Robert E. Kadlec succeeded McMahon as president. At the same time Ronald L. Cliff became chairman of the board. Kadlec, a civil engineering graduate from the University of Toronto, was born in Calgary, Alberta, and joined Inland as chief engineer in 1964. A trustee of the British Columbia Sports Hall of Fame (1987 and 1988), and the current chairman of the Vancouver Board of Trade, Kadlec is past chairman of both the Canadian Gas Association and the Pacific Coast Gas Association, and holds several British Columbia directorships. Kadlec successfully steered his firm through the first year of deregulation, during which time "market pricing" became the key words of the industry.

After 31 years of growth and service, Inland Natural Gas Co. Ltd. is prepared to meet the challenge of change with enthusiasm and confidence.

John A. McMahon, vice-president and president, 1952 to 1972.

Robert E. Kadlec, president and chief executive officer.

TOUCHE ROSS & CO.

Archie Gardner, a chartered accountant, began serving Prince George and the surrounding area from a hotel room more than 40 years ago. A man of vision and imagination, Gardner saw opportunity in the developing province of British Columbia and sought to provide pioneer accounting services in the interior and northwest regions. He spent two to three months per year working from hotel rooms in Prince George, Terrace, and Prince Rupert from 1945 to 1951. At that time an office under the name A.P. Gardner & Co. was opened at 1134 Third Avenue.

Alex Clark, the first resident partner in Prince George, was joined in 1952 by the late Claude Rampton. This was at a time when the city had wooden sidewalks, and student salaries ranged from $125 to $200 per month.

During the 1950s Gardner opened a number of northern offices, building a strong provincial firm. When energies were concentrated on the more populous southern part of the province, all northern offices, with the exception of the fast-growing Prince George office, were sold to local residents.

Prince George experienced exceptional growth in the 1960s and 1970s. From approximately 4,000 in 1951, the city's population grew to number in excess of 70,000. By the 1960s A.P. Gardner & Co. had become one of the largest accounting offices in the city, and it went on to become one of the leading firms in north-central British Columbia. Today Touche Ross services a population of roughly 250,000, which includes Vanderhoof and Burns Lake.

Following Rampton's death in 1961, Harry Beattie became partner in charge, a position he held until 1966. At that time Norman Ratcliffe assumed the position and Jan Ullstrom became a partner in the firm, which at that time was located on Sixth Avenue across from the old health unit. A subsequent move was made to The Inn of the North. The name was changed to Gardner, McDonald & Co. in 1969. Ullstrom became partner in charge in 1973, and two years later the firm merged with the local firm of Willetts, Mcmahon, Thibaudeau & Co. Mark Thibaudeau, George Gibbins, Bill Wright, and Ralph Hagen were admitted as partners to join with Lloyd Irwin, Mel Young, David Ball, Jim Kiddoo, and Ian Petrie.

A move from offices in The Inn of the North to the top floor of the Oxford Building and finally to the Permanent Tower (now Canada Trust Tower) in 1978 was followed by Ball becoming partner in charge a year later. Ullstrom was made senior partner. The year 1980 saw the firm embrace computer technology.

On February 1, 1981, Gardner, McDonald & Co. merged with Touche Ross & Co. Presently the firm has a complement of four partners, offering a combined experience of nearly 100 years, 15 professional staff, and 5 administrative staff—a far cry from the days when Archie Gardner burned the midnight oil in a hotel room.

Touche Ross, presently and through its predecessor firms, A.P. Gardner & Co., and Gardner, McDonald & Co., has served Prince George and Northern British Columbia business communities for more than 40 years.

Touche Ross,

A pioneer accountant to Prince George, Terrace, and Prince Rupert from 1945 to 1951, A.P. Gardner launched a powerful accounting firm that merged with Touche Ross & Co. in 1981.

Canada's first chartered accountancy firm, was founded in Montreal in 1858 and today provides a full range of accounting, audit, tax, trustee, management, and consulting services to the private and public sectors. The firm has in excess of 40 offices in Canada and, through Touche Ross International, operates in 89 countries.

Touche Ross & Co. has four partners (left to right): Lloyd Irwin, Jim Kiddoo, partner in charge David Ball, and senior partner Jan Ullstrom.

B.C. CHEMICALS LTD.

Pulp, the sophisticated material from which paper and paperboard are made, is manufactured by breaking down the cellulose fibres of raw wood by mechanical or chemical means, or a combination of the two. The next step is bleaching, a process requiring chlorine dioxide, which is produced using sodium chlorate.

The establishment of pulp mills in Prince George in the 1960s created a need for sodium chlorate. In order to ensure a reliable supply, B.C. Chemicals was founded in 1965 and production began two

University of North Dakota, his goal was to become a physical education teacher, until an automobile accident in 1959 forced him to change his plans.

An alternate career goal saw Norman accept a position at an Ontario pulp mill, where study and hard work resulted in rapid advancement. An offer to head a new chemical plant in Prince George proved to be a challenge he couldn't help but accept.

Taught by his father to have courage enough to lead even if those who followed him were older

tons was realized in 1988. B.C. Chemicals produces sodium chlorate using graphite bipolar and metal anode technology, the latter being the most efficient in the world.

In addition to supplying sponsor mills with sodium chlorate, used to produce chlorine dioxide, B.C. Chemicals purchases by-products of black liquor soap skimmings from local pulp mills, which, using a batch acidulation process, is manufactured into crude tall oil.

The crude tall oil plant has a rated capacity of 20,000 tons per

years later.

A Joint Venture Chemical Operation owned by Northwood Pulp & Timber Ltd. and Canadian Forest Products, B.C. Chemicals is located on Pulp Mill Road, between Intercontinental Pulp and Prince George Pulp & Paper.

The man behind the daily operations at B.C. Chemicals is H.S. "Hugh" Norman, who came to Prince George from Dryden, Ontario, in 1968 and didn't originally set out to become the manager of a chemical plant in the central interior of British Columbia. Having earned a sports scholarship to the

B.C. Chemicals at its opening in 1967 (left) and as it appears today (right). The company is known for its safe operations, efficiency, and sensitivity toward its employees.

men, Norman has retained that training and passed it on to both his wife and four children, and to the 20 hourly and seven staff employees who make up the B.C. Chemicals family. The company is known for its safe operations, efficiency, and sensitivity toward its personnel.

The sodium chlorate plant's initial capacity was 12,000 tons annually. A rated capacity of 34,000

year. The product is marketed in Japan and the southern United States, where it is further processed into products used in the paint industry, as well as being sold back to paper manufacturers for paper sizing.

Providing a unique service to the pulp and paper industry, B.C. Chemicals Ltd. is a Prince George success story. The secret of this success lies not only in its close proximity to several pulp mills, but in the simple, straightforward management style practiced by president and general manager Hugh Norman.

THE COLLEGE OF NEW CALEDONIA

In 1989 The College of New Caledonia will observe its 20th anniversary. It began operations without referendum approval and without a campus in 1969. In September of that year, using Prince George Senior Secondary School facilities and later merging with the B.C. Vocational School in 1971, The College of New Caledonia became a comprehensive community college offering university, career, trade, and vocational programs. Many events, some controversial, preceded the realization of a college in Prince George.

Prior to 1964 the province of British Columbia had little diversification in higher education. The only postsecondary institutions were the University of British Columbia, its satellite campus in Victoria, and a small private university in Nelson. A limited number of high schools offered grade 13.

Although J.W. Knott developed a plan for a comprehensive college system as early as 1932, it was not until 1958 that an amendment to the Public Schools Act allowed for the establishment of colleges, in affiliation with the University of British Columbia. Not appreciated at the time, Knott's suggestions became reality 35 years later.

The Chant Commission, a 1960 Royal Commission on Education, recommended the addition of grade 13 to all high schools in the province. Proposed as an alternative to establishing postsecondary institutions, the plan did not receive enthusiastic support from either the University of British Columbia or the government.

Two years later University of British Columbia president Dr. John Macdonald presented a report entitled "Higher Education in British Columbia and a Plan for the Future," in which he recommended the establishment of two additional universities in the province and regional colleges in Prince George, the South Cariboo, the Kootenays, and the Okanagan.

The College of New Caledonia's Regional College Committee, created in 1963, was chaired by Dr. A.W. Mooney and included such prominent individuals as Harold Moffat and Galt Wilson from Prince George, Bernice Haggerty from Burns Lake, and Marion Knoerr from Smithers.

Following the presentation of numerous briefs to the Department of Education, the committee finally received approval to hold a plebiscite on June 12, 1967. Making the announcement at a press conference in May at the Simon Fraser Hotel in Prince George, Dr. Mooney also introduced the name of the college. As the proposed institution's region would encompass the same vast region early explorer Simon Fraser had called "New Caledonia," the name was considered appropriate.

The plebiscite was supported in five of the six school districts, with Quesnel failing to give the required 50-percent majority. A later plebiscite held on November 7, 1968, saw residents of that city vote 82 percent in favor of a college. An extensive campaign is credited with the change in attitude.

The first meeting of the college council, consisting of representatives from Burns Lake, McBride, Prince George, Smithers, and Vanderhoof, was held in March 1968 and saw Sam Evans of Prince George appointed chairman.

There followed a busy time during which plans and budgets were drawn up, a capital funding referendum arranged for the fall, and Wolfgang Franke, a former president of the College of Applied Arts and Technology in Sarnia, Ontario, was

Named honorary founding chairmen in 1986, Dr. Alvin Mooney (left) and Harold Moffat display their photographs, which hang in the boardroom of The College of New Caledonia with those of other past chairmen. Courtesy, **The Prince George Citizen**

hired and assumed the position as the college's first president (principal) in September, using a portable building on the grounds of the Prince George Secondary School as an office.

The capital referendum requesting $411,500, held December 7, 1968, which required a 60-percent majority to pass, failed in four of the six districts. Only Quesnel and McBride accepted the proposal with Vanderhoof, Prince George, Smithers, and Burns Lake registering less than the required 60 percent.

Reasons for opposition to the referendum included voters feeling they did not know how much money they would be committing themselves to—they wanted the provincial government to assume more of the cost. Some were uncertain whether or not courses would be transferable to the universities, whether quality instruction would be obtained, whether there would be sufficient enrolment, and whether the curriculum would suit the needs of the community. Also clouding the issue was the existence of Prince George College, a private parochial college in the city, leading some to ask why another college was needed.

Above left: Wolfgang Franke, the college's first principal. Franke was formerly a president of the College of Applied Arts and Technology in Sarnia, Ontario.

Above center: Dr. Frederick J. Speckeen, principal, 1970 to 1978. During Speckeen's tenure The College of New Caledonia was united with the British Columbia Vocational School.

Above right: Charles J. McCaffray, principal since 1978, directs a faculty of 145 members.

The council voted to proceed, requesting operating funds from the school boards and taxpayers. The first classes were held in September 1969, and official opening ceremonies took place in October of the same year.

Dr. Frederick J. Speckeen replaced Wolfgang Franke as principal in July 1970, and the college was amalgamated with the B.C. Vocational School (current campus site) a year later. The B.C. Vocational School had opened in 1962 and at the time of amalgamation had more than 250 full-time students in more than a dozen programs ranging from bookkeeping to welding, heavy equipment operation to dental assisting.

At first portable structures were used in conjunction with the main building, and in 1974 the provincial government spent more than $10 million on a major build-ing expansion, adding a permanent library and shop facilities, a food-service facility, and more classrooms. The expansion was completed in 1977. In February 1982 the province approved in excess of $2 million for the completion of the existing third floor of the college's main campus. The addition provided new laboratory space for chemistry, forestry, drafting, and computer information services; classroom space for Adult Basic Education; and office space for the Continuing Education Division. A more recent expansion, a Dental Training Clinic, was opened early in 1988.

The year 1975 saw the first satellite campus opened in Vanderhoof. Burns Lake followed a year later, with Mackenzie and Quesnel satellites opened in 1979.

Charles McCaffray replaced Dr. Speckeen as principal in 1978, and today directs a full-time faculty of 145 and 130 part-time instructors. The original faculty numbered 20.

Beginning with a basic univer-sity transfer program, the institution added vocational/trade programs in 1971. Today The College of New Caledonia offers a wide range of courses from heavy-duty mechanics to dental hygiene, cook training and early childhood education to degree completion opportunities (through various degree-granting institutions) in education, arts and science, commerce, and business. The student population, which stood at 516 in 1969, has increased to nearly 3,000.

The college campus is accessible to the handicapped and, with an enrolment of 120 physically and mentally challenged individuals, has one of the largest special education divisions in the British Columbia college system.

Since 1967 The College of New Caledonia Board, with chairmen S. Evans, G. Wilson, R. Affleck, F. Dingwall, J. Prichard, R. Rushant, A. Howard Gibbon, D. Flynn, R. Stewart, and J. Blunt, has guided the growth and change of the institution.

The early history of the college was forged with foresight, dedication, and a good measure of controversy. While the government provided direction and support, the College of New Caledonia owes its existence to the many committed individuals in the community who, in the face of many challenges and setbacks, had the strength and vision to make it a reality.

The Dental Training Clinic, which opened in February 1988.

NORTHWOOD PULP AND TIMBER LIMITED

Pulp mills are now a major factor in the economy of the North.

While commonly thought of as relatively new to this area, pulp mills were being considered as far back as the early 1900s, when a group of farsighted entrepreneurs sought necessary funding and government approval to use the rich forest area along the Fraser River east of Prince George for pulp production.

During the Great War of 1914-1918, a group headed by F.P. Jones of Montreal and Angus McLean of Bathurst, New Brunswick, acquired large timber holdings along the Fraser River east of Prince George with the intention of building a pulp mill. Failure to reach an agreement on royalties with the provincial government stalled proceedings for a time. Almost a decade later royalties were adjusted, and roughly one million dollars was spent on surveys and site acquisitions. The death of McLean, the serious illness of Jones, and the economic slump of 1929 ended

Northwood's expanded pulp mill operation, located just north of Prince George.

the dream of the Fraser River Pulp and Paper Co.

The dream began to come true in 1961, when Noranda bought a number of local, small sawmills and timber-harvesting rights along the "east line," belonging to National Forest Products, with the intention of combining inefficient small mills to get economy of scale. However, as mills were added a new problem developed.

"We saw pulp mills as a solution to a gigantic waste-disposal problem at first," says Adam Zimmerman, Northwood's founding president and current chairman of Noranda Forest Inc. Only about one-half of each cubic metre of wood entering a sawmill becomes lumber. Pulp mills can use most of what would otherwise be waste.

In the process of acquiring mills, the company purchased, among others, Sinclair Spruce Lumber Company, Upper Fraser Spruce Mills Ltd., Fichtner Lumber Co., Hansard Lumber Co., Church Sawmills Ltd., and Eagle Lake Sawmills at Giscome and Shelley.

Where hundreds of small-scale logging and lumber firms once

struggled, a major integrated forest products company operates today. With sawmills, a plywood plant, a waterboard operation, and what is considered the world's largest single bleached softwood kraft pulpmill, Northwood Pulp and Timber Limited currently produces forest-related products for shipment around the world.

This consolidation included much of the history of the North, echoing the dream of the Fraser River Pulp and Paper Co.

In discussing logging methods and the lifestyle of the early inhabitants along the east line, longtime employee Horst Sander, president, who replaced managing director Carl Frantz in 1979, says he is most impressed with "the incredible innovation of people." Isolated and totally dependent on rail transportation, they created communities and made lasting contributions to the growth and history of the central interior.

To relive the early days on the

Northwood's small log sawmill, located approximately eight kilometres north of Prince George.

Above: Ken Watson, retired director of the nursery, examines the first crop of seedlings produced at Northwood's Forest Centre.

Left: A feller-buncher harvests a Lodgepole pine near Vama Creek.

east line, one has to talk to people such as Doug Little, senior vice-president/forest operations at Northwood, who worked as a forester at Sinclair Mills. Little, in recalling early road conditions, describes the Giscome "highway": "You had to take your own boards along, to plank your way out of tough spots."

In 1964 Noranda joined with the Mead Corporation of Dayton, Ohio, to form Northwood Pulp Limited (later changed to Northwood Pulp and Timber Limited). In 1965 Northwood had the necessary tree farm licences, the Mead group had the pulp production and marketing expertise, and that spring pulp mill construction commenced.

This was also a year of tragedy. On July 8 a regularly scheduled Canadian Pacific Airlines DC6-B exploded and crashed in the 100 Mile House area, less than

The first mobile unit used at McLean Sawmill. Photo circa 1937

one hour from Prince George. All aboard, including Northwood's vice-president and general manager Keith Eadie and his wife, plant manager Norman Harvey, and production manager Don Gaitens, died in the crash. On a house-hunting expedition, the Northwood executives were to have moved to Prince George later that summer.

The pulp mill start-up highlighted 1966. Also that year, following the acquisition of Eagle Lake Saw-

mills with operations at Giscome and Shelley, Northwood consolidated its five tree farm licences into one. An experiment in summer logging proved successful with 36,000 units harvested. Eagle Lake was later closed and the townsite dismantled in 1974.

Northwood's pulp mill, located within the northeast boundaries of the City of Prince George, produces prime-grade bleached softwood kraft pulp and ships it worldwide, where it is turned into high-quality printing, writing, and business papers; postage stamps; currency; and tissues.

Since its start-up in 1966, the mill has benefited from a policy of continuous technical updating and capital improvement, establishing its reputation as an efficient

141

producer of premium-quality bleached softwood kraft pulp.

Pulp production involves breaking down the cellulose fibres of raw wood and bleaching the resulting brownstock pulp. A reliable supply of chemicals for this process was assured through the establishment of B.C. Chemicals Ltd., a joint-venture operation with Prince George Pulp & Paper.

The original design provided for the pulp mill to be "twinned"—or doubled in production capacity—when economic conditions were right. The company decided to launch the expansion in 1979. It was completed three years later. With a design capacity of 1,450 metric tons per day, Northwood's pulp mill now provides employment for 650 people.

Northwood's wood products division today operates four sawmills in the north-central interior, producing 700 million fbm, which is approximately 45 railcars of lumber per day or 12,000 railcars per year, enough to frame some 86,000 homes. Mostly kiln-dried dimension lumber, it is sold in Canada, the United States, the United Kingdom, Europe, Japan, and Australia. Rough green lumber is shipped to the United Kingdom and Europe.

Through technology and modernization programs, Northwood's four sawmills are now specialized to make the most efficient use of the widely varied sizes of logs harvested.

The facilities range in size and diversity from the large Houston complex (formerly Bulkey Valley Forest Industries), which employs some 340 people and is equipped to handle virtually any log size in the area, to the Shelley mill, which employs roughly 120 people and produces a variety of specialty grades and cuts, largely for the offshore

Horst G. Sander, president.

market. The others are a small-log mill at Prince George employing 175 and a modernized general processing mill at Upper Fraser employing 235.

Most of the wood entering the sawmills is utilized. Solid wood not manufactured into lumber is converted to chips—approximately 500,000 tons per year from Northwood's mills alone—to feed the pulp mill. Even bark and sawdust are used. Known as hog fuel, it is used to generate process steam for the pulp mill and 80 percent of the electrical requirements of the pulp mill and the Prince George sawmill. Together the sawmill operations employ approximately one-half of Northwood's total work force.

Further diversification of the company and more efficient wood use were achieved through the purchase of North Central Plywoods Ltd. in 1980.

Year-round access to logging areas and the Canadian National Railway's main line is provided by the construction of a two-lane bridge across the Fraser River.

J.D. "Doug" Little, senior vice-president/forest operations.

One lane for rail traffic and the other for truck traffic provides access to Northwood's harvest and sawmill operations in the East.

Northwood has set a high standard for forest management in the industry. Regeneration of the forest was an early consideration. In June 1967 Northwood's one-millionth seedling was planted, the 50-millionth in 1984, and in June 1988 the 100-millionth seedling was planted.

The new Forest Act of 1979 permitted the development of private nurseries to assist in the growing demand for seedlings. Northwood's forest centre, near the mill site, was completed and the first crop of seedlings was planted in 1982; today it produces some 10 million seedlings each year.

Since its earliest beginnings Northwood Pulp and Timber Limited has made deliberate progress toward full integration of its operations. That goal has been realized by maximizing the utilization of raw materials, minimizing waste, and replenishing the forest resource.

THE PRINCE GEORGE REGIONAL HOSPITAL

Prince George's first hospital was a rough structure described by historian F.E. Runnalls as a large tent where new mothers would take their babies and sacks of potatoes to bed to keep both from freezing.

The first doctor, Dr. D.B. Lazier, arrived on the BX sternwheeler in 1910 and had as his hospital a log building in South Fort George. During epidemics, facilities were expanded with tents. Dr. Lazier was assisted by Miss B.A. Fry, the first registered nurse in the area.

In 1911 George Hammond, developer of Central Fort George, was instrumental in the construction of a four-bed, wood-frame hospital in that area in which Drs. Hugh McSorely and Cecil Swenerton cared for the sick and injured. It is said to be the first British Columbia hospital located north of Quesnel.

The influenza epidemic of 1912 hastened construction of the Grand Trunk Pacific Railway Hospital in the Island Cache, and the worldwide influenza outbreak in 1918 brought about the building of the 35-bed Pine Manor on the site of the present Simon Fraser Lodge. It was there that Dr. Carl Ewert and Dr. Eddie Lyon practiced. Dr. Ewert's son Robert, a surgeon, currently practices in Prince George.

Following World War II Prince George inherited the military hospital, which it soon outgrew, and in 1960 the 125-bed Prince George Regional Hospital was opened. During the next two decades hospital expansion kept pace with the growth of the district.

During the 1960s and 1970s rapid population growth placed extreme pressure on the hospital,

The Prince George Regional Hospital at its present site in 1988.

and during peak periods a fifth bed was set up in four-bed wards; lounges were converted to patient areas; and beds were set up in corridors.

Necessary additions in the early 1960s include completion of the fourth floor and construction of the fifth-floor pediatric unit. The year 1982 saw completion of areas for medical imaging, operating rooms, day-care surgery, labor/delivery, post-anesthetic recovery, stores, Jubilee Lodge (a 72-bed extended-care facility), emergency, outpatients, admitting, and laboratory. Aided by a local telethon, a therapy pool was constructed and a portion of a 26-bed rehabilitation unit also came into service in 1988. Prince George Regional Hospital presently has 296 acute care beds, 72 extended care beds, 37 chemical dependency beds, and 44 bassinets.

Operated under the direction of a 10-member board and an executive director, the Prince George Regional Hospital has the services of 112 physicians: 45 general practitioners, 63 specialists in many fields, and 4 permanent locum tenens.

The year 1988 marked the 65th anniversary of the auxiliary to the

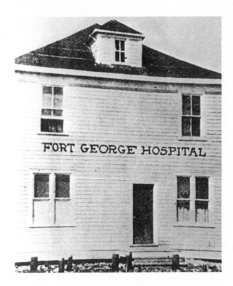

The four-bed, wood-frame Central Fort George Hospital was developed by George Hammond.

Prince George Regional Hospital. Originally involved in providing necessities, which included potatoes and bed linens, the auxiliary currently provides an in-house volunteer service and raises funds that help supply sophisticated equipment.

From a makeshift shack on the banks of the Fraser River, the Prince George Regional Hospital has grown into a fully accredited regional referral hospital.

THE PRINCE GEORGE CITIZEN

Following several colorful predecessors, the first issue of *The Citizen* was published May 17, 1916.

Between 1909 and 1916 the *Tribune,* the *Herald,* the *Post,* the *Daily News,* and the *Star* all began publication. Some folded almost as quickly as they began. On May 17, 1916, Louis D. Taylor, later to become mayor of Vancouver and set the record for total years in that office, published the first edition of *The Citizen.* By 1917 the *Star* had been amalgamated with *The Citizen,* followed by the *Leader* a short time later.

For more than 30 years *The Citizen* continued as the sole news-

brief appearance in 1958, followed by *The Prince George Progress,* which continued to publish until 1970.

Under the ownership of W.B. Milner's Northwest Publications, *The Citizen* changed its address in 1963 from a location on Quebec Street (where Zellers Parkade is now) to its present location at 150 Brunswick Street and became the first daily newspaper in Canada to switch to offset print technology.

In the spring of 1969 *The Citizen* was purchased by and became a division of Southam Inc., which now has 15 divisions (newspapers). The change of ownership had obvious advantages, including access

launched the *North Star* with a commitment to publish daily, but the paper ceased publication a year later. Other short-lived publications include *The Prospect,* which began publishing in December 1975, and *The Spruce Needle,* in August 1982.

In 1976 *The Citizen* was again experiencing growing pains, and a large addition was constructed for the editorial department. *The Citizen* embraced the new newspaper technology and computerized in 1982. On October 20, 1984, it began publishing on Saturday. Circulation swelled to 24,000. A $100,000 renovation project was carried out during the winter of 1985-1986, coin-

paper in the community. During this time the paper was purchased by Harry Perry, for many years Liberal member of the provincial legislature for Fort George and speaker of the British Columbia legislature.

In 1974 Perry sold the newspaper to three of his employees—Harry Kennedy, Cliff Warner, and Nestor Izowski. They began publishing three times per week and by 1954 had increased weekly circulation to 2,300.

Bought by the Citizen Publishers and Printers Ltd. on November 19, 1956, publication of *The Citizen* was increased to five days per week on September 3, 1957.

The Prince George Echo made a

Left: W.L. Griffith, publisher, January 1, 1966, to July 31, 1970.

Left center: J.F. Evans, publisher, August 1, 1970, to September 30, 1980.

Right center: B.W. Stone, publisher, October 1, 1980, to July 31, 1987.

Right: A.J. McNair, publisher, August 1, 1987, to present.

to Southam News Services. Today Southam and Canadian Press news services, stock prices, and photographs are received with a four-metre dish aimed at the ANIK-2 satellite.

In May 1970 the late Ben Ginter

ciding with the 70th anniversary of the paper.

Others who have guided the destiny of *The Citizen* are publishers R.A. Renwick, H.G.T. Perry, Terry Hammond, Lew Griffiths, John Evans, and Bryson Stone. Current publisher Alastair McNair came to *The Citizen* from *Pacific Press* in Vancouver. Longtime editor Tony Skae retired in 1984 and was replaced by present editor Roy Nagel.

Throughout its 70-plus years, *The Prince George Citizen* has followed a pattern of growth that paralleled the community, expanding and adapting to the changing face of Prince George.

NOVAK BROS. LTD.
DUNKLEY LUMBER LTD.

It takes a special kind of person to turn a chicken farm into a sawmill. That's how the late Bill Dunkley created Dunkley Lumber Ltd.

His original intention had been to sell the mill, but his realization of the lumber potential of the area prompted him to put the mill to work in 1951.

Dunkley and siblings Ernie, Tim, Bessie, and Phyllis were joined by their brother, David, in 1954. The elder Dunkleys, Lily and George, arrived two years later.

Dunkley Lumber quickly became a small town, with 50 houses for families, and bunkhouses for single workers and those with families in Prince George. The centre of activity, a large building with a general store on the first floor and office above, still serves the unique community.

When the mill changed hands in 1977, Bessie agreed to stay on for six months. She's still there, as well as her brother David and many more. Mobile homes have, for the most part, replaced the

houses built in the 1950s, and vastly improved roads and vehicles have brought the city a lot closer, but much of the old atmosphere and neighborliness remain.

In the early 1950s the trip from Dunkley Lumber to Prince George was not the easy drive it is today; vehicles of that period were often defeated by the seven miles of muddy dirt road leading to the gravel highway.

During spring breakup and rainy weather it was often necessary for vehicles to be pulled by tractors over the seven miles of muddy road to the highway.

The only thing stopping the railroad from reaching Prince George was "60 miles of beaver dams and swamps," according to a premier who refused to extend the line. This meant the north was stopped from development because everything had to be trucked to the end of the track at Quesnel.

Finally, in 1952, the rails went north. The Pacific & Great Eastern, now the British Columbia Railway, cut across the Dunkley property. This provided an alternative to costly trucking of the lumber.

The highway took longer. It

was 1960 before Highway 97 South replaced the old Cariboo Highway. It passed beside Dunkley, thus ending the company's nearly 10 years of isolation.

In 1977, after more than a quarter-century of ownership, the Dunkley family sold the mill to the Novak family of Prince George. The four Novak brothers, all former loggers, immediately embarked on a major renovation/modernization program.

Today logs, cants, and boards pass through electronic scanners that feed computers with the most accurate information to determine the best possible cuts. This advanced technology is also used for trimming, sorting, and packaging of lumber.

Henry Novak, the president of Dunkley Lumber Ltd., observes: "Our people and high-tech equipment are responsible for keeping us competitive in the world market. By supplying our customers with a top-quality product, we all benefit."

This building, with a store on the first floor and a corporate office above, has been the centre of activity at Dunkley for more than 30 years. Courtesy, **The Prince George Citizen**

The Novak family (back row, left to right): Joe, Max, Cveta, Henry, and Tony. Front row (left to right): Metod, Terezija, Max Sr., and Ciril. The Novaks bought the mill from the Dunkley family in 1977.

PRINCE GEORGE WAREHOUSING CO. LTD.
NORTHERN INTERIOR FASTFRATE LTD.

The Assman family has a long history in Prince George. John Assman, Sr., came to the area from Bordon, Saskatchewan, in 1914. He and his wife, Maria, raised a family of 10 in a house built on Assman's Slough, the site most recently occupied by Ginter Construction.

In 1922 he built the Assman Block on Third Avenue, and opened a grocery and feed store on the main floor. The store's cold room, topped with glass bricks, extended out under the sidewalk and was an ideal spot for ripening bananas.

The business suffered a severe financial reversal during the Depression and was taken over by John's son Harold and Oscar Bouch. It later became the Crystal Market.

Sometime later John Assman, Jr., went to work for Karl Anderson, driving a truck between Prince George and Vancouver, distributing general freight and beer. It was on one of these trips that he and his wife were married in Vancouver. Returning with a load of potatoes, they were stopped at Hixon, where the flooding creek had washed out a section of road. Learning of their plight, Spike Enemark

This building, pictured in 1922, belonged to Herb Assman and housed Karl Anderson's Panama Variety store (below).

went to Hixon and helped carry three tons of potatoes across the swollen stream and load them onto his truck. The shipment reached Prince George on schedule, and the young couple experienced a memorable honeymoon trip.

Following Karl Anderson's death in 1957, Assman assumed the beer distribution business, and Prince George Warehousing Co. Ltd. was born. At this time Herb Assman joined the business, becoming president upon his father's

retirement in 1971.

A brash young businessman, Herb Assman recognized the need for money for expansion and, being a born risk-taker, went ahead and borrowed it. The ambitious expansion plan, carried out over 10 years, saw the construction of three major warehouses and the addition of a considerable number of trucks and amount of related equipment. Northern Interior Fastfrate Ltd., a division of Prince George Warehousing Co. Ltd., was established in 1978 and began regular service to Vancouver in 1980, daily service to Prince Rupert in 1986, and daily service to Dawson Creek and Fort St. John in 1987. Using a fleet of 80 trucks and trailers, it offers 10 schedules per day to 1,853 customers. With branches in Vancouver, Edmonton, and Dawson Creek and agents in Terrace, Fastfrate trucks travel to points as distant as Edmonton, Calgary, Prince Rupert, and the Yukon border.

A staff of 100 co-ordinates warehousing and distribution. Several million pounds of freight pass through the facilities every day. Of course, brewery distribution is as important now as it was in Karl Anderson's day.

Today Herb Assman operates

Photo courtesy, Fort George Museum

a modern, successful warehousing and freighting business. A vital man, he's very involved in his family, his business, and his community. In discussing family and corporate history, he dwells on certain details, such as his mother, Kate's, family, the Blackburns, early Aleza Lake settlers. He also remembers the Assman Slough, where in the early 1920s youngsters learned to skate, located on the site of the former Ginter Construction yards on First Avenue. In 1987 Assman returned the property to family

ownership, and the following year new office and terminal buildings were constructed where his grandfather built his house in 1914. The new home of Prince George Warehousing and Interior Fastfrate will reflect the growth and success of this local company.

On the subject of being in business, he says of the 1960s and 1970s, "Things were easier then . . . we had the luxury of time." With a faraway look in his eye he recalls, "The day Harry Loder came to town." Loder was a very colorful businessman, alderman, and com-

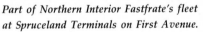

Part of Northern Interior Fastfrate's fleet at Spruceland Terminals on First Avenue.

munity worker who was associated with Karl Anderson and John Assman.

According to Assman, freighting is, "The toughest league to get into. Competing with multinational carriers is difficult. People in Prince George and other northern centres are receivers. It's our responsibility to get them their freight as fast and as economically as possible. That's why our head office is here." He takes considerable pride in the fact that his company is 100-percent Canadian.

Assman and his wife, Julie, have two daughters and a son. Named for his great-grandfather and grandfather, son John is active in the business, assuring it being in the family for another generation.

He has a good teacher. His father says, "When I started building this company to the independent operation it is now, I started from zero. I learned by doing. I know how to fill a truck and an empty warehouse."

The entire 1961 fleet of Herb Assman's Prince George Warehousing.

147

DERON FOREST TECHNIK LTD.

While technology has dramatically changed the logging industry, one process has remained constant: Trees still must be harvested one at a time. It is how they are processed that makes the difference.

The introduction of harvesting smaller trees demanded a different way to process them, and tree processors were introduced to replace chain saws. The first machine snipped the tree. Trees were then brought to a landing where workers with power saws limbed and bucked them to length. This process was slow, and the quality was poor. With the new computerized mills a demand for accurate measurements and clean logs was created. The search for a more flexible, more economical machine began.

In 1985 two young businessmen, aware of changes in the industry and the demands for more efficient logging equipment, formed Deron Forest Technik Ltd. and began importing a revolutionary tree processor from Austria.

Deryl Truman and Ron Gobin formed Deron Forest Technik Ltd. in Prince George and introduced the virtually unknown Austrian-manufactured Steyr KP40 tree processor or delimber to the market. At first considered to be little more than a toy, the Steyr's performance has proven detractors wrong, and it is now considered to be the finest computerized processor on the market.

Truman and Gobin admit their venture took considerable courage and that some thought it a bit of a gamble. Acceptance of their remarkable machine was almost immediate. Seven machines were sold in the first months of operation and 12 in 1986. The following year in excess of 40 machines were placed, and sales are predicted to surpass 50 for 1988. Demand for the Steyr KP40 and the larger KP60, introduced in 1987, continues to grow; the entire first shipment of KP60 processors was presold.

Deron's success is evidenced by the fact that the exclusive marketing territory for Steyr has expanded to include British Columbia, Alberta, Saskatchewan, Idaho, Montana, Washington, and Oregon. Truman and Gobin's expansion plan indicates the next move will be into the Maritimes.

Aggressive promotion, on-site

In 1987, to keep pace with its own rapid growth, Deron Forest Technik Ltd. moved to a larger facility with areas for display, demonstration, sales, and service.

demonstrations, efficient servicing, and adequate parts inventory have served to establish Deron Forest Technik as a leader in the industry.

Seeing the Steyr equipment in action is an education in itself, showing the viewer just how much logging methods have changed. Simplicity of design combined with computerized efficiency have produced a processor capable of limbing, bucking, sorting, and decking. The result is a precision-cut, quality piece of timber. The low initial cost and consistent high-quality production combine to allow competition in the world market.

The versatile KP40 can be mounted on all hydraulic excavators, self-propelled loaders, and track-type or rubber-tired vehicles capable of delivering approximately 100 horsepower. Controls consist of a computerized display programming and operating unit.

The average output of approximately 120 trees per hour, sized from seven centimetres to 46 centimetres, is something old-time loggers who waded through snow in freezing weather carrying a heavy chain saw never dreamed possible.

An efficient servicing department is one of the many components contributing to the success of Deron Forest Technik Ltd.

Seven different lengths can be programmed into the computerized measuring device, and the capacity to pre-set top diameter size using a micro-limit switch distinguishes the high-tech system that delivers near-perfect wood from 'stump to dump'—a term used by loggers to describe the process of taking raw trees from the bush to the final destination at sawmill or pulp mill.

The process is precise and simple. During operation the machine is lowered with opened grapples onto the tree. Two lower grapple knives and two grapple arms are closed, pressing the tree against the upper front knives and steel roller feed chain. Forward movement of the tree is done automatically with no slipping and minimum wood damage. The tree is then cut to specified computer length automatically by a circular saw.

The manufacturer, Steyr-Daimler-Puch of Austria, was founded nearly 125 years ago, and, in addition to being the manufacturer of forestry equipment, is

the dominant builder of vehicles in that country.

The years of research and development and traditional European craftsmanship, combined with Deron's hydraulic expertise and dedication to the product, give Steyr logging equipment the rugged endurance demanded by North American logging operators.

The rapid growth of Deron Forest Technik necessitated a move in 1987 from the small quarters at 2019 First Avenue to a larger facility, featuring areas for display, demonstration, sales, and service, at 1204 Pacific Street in the BCR Industrial Park in Prince George.

Truman, Gobin, and a growing staff are working hard to keep up with the success of the Steyr KP40 and 60. As the largest dealer in Steyr's Forest Division, the firm is part of the new history of logging, providing a product that makes a difference in the woods.

A Prince George success story, Deron Forest Technik Ltd. is destined to play an increasingly important role in the changing forest industry, locally and throughout North America.

DOMTAR CHEMICALS GROUP WOOD PRESERVING DIVISION

Wherever one lives in Canada, Domtar may not be far away. The corporation operates in all provinces except Prince Edward Island and Newfoundland. Reading a newspaper, shaking salt on food, opening up a shipping container, adding a room to the house, riding on a train, or receiving power or telephone service via a utility pole probably means coming into contact with Domtar.

Domtar was born as The Dominion Tar and Chemical Company Limited in 1903. A subsidiary of a tar-distillation and wood-treating firm in London, England, it first opened a plant in Sydney, Nova Scotia. In 1929 a group of Canadian investors bought all the assets of the British company and incorporated under Canadian law. During the 1960s the name was simplified to Domtar Limited, and in 1978 to Domtar Inc.

Domtar has grown into a truly Canadian corporation with more than 90 percent of its common shares registered in Canadian names. James H. Smith, president and chief executive officer, oversees the firm's far-flung operations from its head office in Montreal.

Domtar's Wood Preserving Division, made up of nine plants, one of which is located in Prince George, is the major producer of utility poles and railway ties in Canada.

One of the first to locate in the P.G.E. Industrial Park (now the BCR Industrial Park), Domtar purchased and leased a total of 122 heavily wooded acres four miles south of town. After the timber was cleared, construction on the plant began in 1960, and upon completion a year later, treating operations commenced. The original staff numbered five, compared to the present 35.

While Domtar's Prince George wood-preserving plant was built primarily to treat ties for the P.G.E. Railway, production soon expanded to include other items.

The pole-peeling operation acquired earlier from Northern Wood Preservers Limited at Otway was moved to the new site in 1962, and five years later an Augustine Pole Peeler was installed, making possible production of utility poles, piling, construction poles, and posts.

The original treating cylinder was extended to allow additional treating capacity in 1964, and 11 years later a second cylinder was installed. Using oil-borne preservatives, Domtar now supplies ties to both the BCR and CN, and utility poles to B.C. Hydro, B.C. Telephone, Alberta Power, and other companies as far east as Manitoba. Lodgepole pine is readily available in the area and lends itself to pole production.

A relative newcomer to Prince George is Andrew Henry, Domtar's plant manager. He has a lot of experience to call on—millworker Maurice Van Caeseele has been on the job for 32 years, chief engineer Owen Edwards has 22 years' experience, and yard foreman Jim Miller has logged 26 years. Andrew is justifiably proud of Domtar-Prince George's production, pollution control, and safety records. The plant has received a number of safety awards, including many Zero Frequency awards from the Council of Forest Industries.

Domtar is part of the community and recognizes its corporate responsibilities, taking an active interest in local affairs, maintaining contact with community leaders, and funding causes and cultural activities.

People in Prince George come in contact with Domtar in a very real way.

An early photograph of the 122-acre Domtar site, surrounded by heavy timber. One of the first firms to locate in the BCR Industrial Park, Domtar is surrounded by industrial neighbors.

Today the Domtar Wood Preserving Division covers the large site with an operation that supplies ties to two railways and utility poles to clients as far east as Manitoba.

OVERWAITEA FOODS

R.C. Kidd founded Overwaitea Foods in New Westminster on March 8, 1915, with an investment of only $500 and a unique approach to service.

In that first store was established a merchandising concept that became the company name. As a bonus to attract customers, Kidd packaged high-quality Indian and Ceylon blended teas with 18 ounces for the price of 16 ounces, developing a reputation for selling overweight tea—hence the name Overwaitea.

A second store, opened in Nanaimo in 1918, launched the Overwaitea chain.

"If you go to the store with the big teapot on the front, you'll get a piece of watermelon." This was the message passed along to children in 1934, when Jack Nicholson (elected mayor in 1944) opened the first Overwaitea in Prince George. Located in the 200 block on George Street, just down from the McDonald Hotel, the store's first employees were Edgar Jeffries and Ted Gibbins. Offering dry groceries and a limited line of cellar-type produce—potatoes, carrots, and onions—the store did not carry fresh meat. Nor did it sell tobacco, as R.C. Kidd did not permit smoking in his stores, maintaining it impaired the quality of the tea and butter.

The famous green teapot, proclaiming "Overwaitea is Good Tea," adorned two locations on Third Avenue before an 11,000-square-foot store opened at 1601 Victoria Street on November 24, 1959, offering, in addition to the traditional grocery line, meats, produce, and dairy products.

The success of the Victoria Street outlet and the growth of the city prompted the company to open a second store of 14,000 square feet in the Spruceland Shop-

The famous green Overwaitea teapot that adorned storefronts in the early days. Replicas of these teapots are now cherished keepsakes.

ping Centre in June 1961. The late Doug Trigg, manager of the Victoria Street store since 1961, opened and managed the new store until his retirement in 1980 ended a 27-year career with Overwaitea. The Spruceland Store marked the beginning of a succession of new stores in Prince George.

In 1968 the Overwaitea operation was purchased by the Pattison Group, and in the past 20 years it has grown by some 300 percent, while maintaining the people-oriented philosophy of Robert Kidd.

April 23, 1969, saw the opening of a new 18,000-square-foot store at 1601 Victoria Street, replacing the one built 10 years earlier. Additional parking space was gained by removing the old building.

On May 15, 1974, Overwaitea opened its third outlet, a 17,000-square-foot store in the Hart Shopping Centre.

In 1976 increasing population again made it necessary to replace the Victoria Street store—this time with a 27,000-square-foot building fronting on Spruce Street that still serves city customers.

The fourth Overwaitea outlet was opened in the College Heights area on October 5, 1978, and proved popular with the huge residential population west of the city.

The Hart area was burgeoning, too, and December 10, 1984, saw the opening of a 37,000-square-foot Overwaitea facility built next to the old store in the Hart Shopping Centre.

A series of events in 1985 led to replacing the Spruceland outlet with a 55,000-square-foot mega-store. The original store closed March 9, 1985, and the operation, relocated in a vacant grocery store in the same centre, opened for business two days later. The new store, offering 25,000 lines with a product mix that in addition to basic grocery, meat, produce, and dairy departments includes bakery, books, housewares, bulk foods, and a deli, opened May 2, 1986.

Throughout Overwaitea's 54-year history in Prince George, the company has grown with the community. As "B.C.'s Very Own Food People," Overwaitea Foods takes pride in the province and the people it serves. The company's history in Prince George in many ways mirrors its history throughout British Columbia.

LINDEN FABRICATING & ENGINEERING P.G. LTD.

In 1959 Bruno Lindenblatt, recently arrived from Germany and speaking very little English, found work as a logger in Alberta. While mastering a new language and becoming accustomed to the different climate and customs, Lindenblatt recognized the great potential and opportunities of his adopted country.

Bruno Lindenblatt, president.

Trained as a millwright in Germany, Lindenblatt soon found work as a mechanic working in sawmills in British Columbia, an occupation that led to modifying and improving existing equipment. Realizing he could be designing and building more efficient equipment to keep pace with the changes taking place in the industry was the first step toward forming his own fabricating company.

On April 28, 1972, Lindenblatt and his wife, Ursula, founded Linden Welding & Fabricating Ltd. in Quesnel, British Columbia. The first year saw six employees put on the payroll. The process of becoming established involved repair, maintenance, and minor fabrication for sawmill equipment in the area, in contrast to current production, which involves turnkey projects that are a complete supply-and-install package to the sawmill industry, employing up to 350 workers.

Today Linden Welding & Fabricating Ltd. in Quesnel has a capacity of approximately 250 tons a month, operating in a 14,000-square-foot building. Sophisticated equipment includes an Omada hydraulic saw with 22-inch capacity, a 200-ton press, an electric eye multitorch, portable line-boring equipment, four milling machines, and four overhead cranes. Monty McKelvie is in charge of the Quesnel plant.

In the 1970s the sawmill industry underwent a significant change: In response to demands from world markets, competition increased. Mill owners had to optimize their operations with modern-day technology and equipment. Another, perhaps far more significant reason for sawmill reconstruction, was the smaller trees being cut and processed. The old equipment could not handle the smaller-size logs. An era was ending; computerization was a reality.

Lindenblatt expanded his company; Linden Fabricating & Engineering P.G. Ltd. was established in Prince George in March 1981. Located at 9368 Milwaukee Way in the BCR Industrial Park, the 25,000-square-foot building, equipped with four overhead cranes, a 200-ton press, a structural saw with 30-inch capacity, sandblasting, and inside painting facilities, offers a shop capacity of 400 tons per month. High-technology changes in the industry affected Linden as well; in order to remain competitive in the supply of structural steel for sawmill construction, a computerized drilling line was installed. Garry Larsen oversees the Prince George operation.

As area sawmills continued to modify and replace, the third division in the Linden group, Linden Sawmill Construction Ltd., was created and operates under the direction of Jim McManus.

The Linden group, in addition to serving the forest industry, is involved in community life as well, supporting the arts, sports, and a number of local projects. The man behind Linden Welding & Fabricating Ltd., Linden Fabricating & Engineering P.G. Ltd., and Linden Sawmill Construction Ltd., Bruno Lindenblatt, is a robust, enthusiastic businessman who, when time permits, enjoys travel and racquetball.

EAST FRASER LOGGING LTD.

Chris Winther directs his highly successful logging, lumber, and other operations from an office in downtown Prince George. No stranger to the area, Winther emigrated from Denmark and came to Prince George in 1951. Raised on a farm with five brothers and four sisters, he brought with him the Danish love for the land and appreciation of wood.

Together with brothers Paul and Eric and associate Ivan Beach, Winther formed East Fraser Logging in 1956. Located at Mile 48 on the CN East Line, near Penny Spruce Mills, the logging camp was reached by crossing the ice in the winter and by boat in the summer. Logs were cut during the winter and in the spring floated down the river and caught in booms by the various mills.

In the early days logging was seasonal work. East Fraser had as many as 150 men working at one time. Today's sophisticated equipment results in more volume with less manpower. "There were more opportunities in the old days," says Winther. "Deals were made with a handshake. There's more volume now, but more risk, too."

Winther recalls that East Fraser Logging was, like other woods operations in the area, totally dependent on the railway. A lantern was put out to stop the train that went through at 2 a.m. for everything from someone going into town for a visit to transporting a sick or injured person to the hospital in Prince George. Fortunately there were no serious injuries during the two years East Fraser operated in the Penny area.

However, there was an incident involving East Fraser's first crawler-type tractor. Delivered by rail, it had to be transported across the river to the logging camp. The tractor was loaded onto a large raft, built for the occasion. With line attached, the craft was launched. A few feet from shore disaster struck. The current caught the raft on the low side and it was in imminent danger of sinking. A quick-thinking logger, inspired by a vision of the tractor settling into the mud at the bottom of the river, cut the line and the listing craft, carried by the current, came to rest harmlessly against the riverbank a short distance down stream. A second attempt proved successful. The mechanization of East Fraser Logging had begun.

In 1958 East Fraser secured a contract logging for Meirs Brothers (Lorne, Dick, Boyd, and Richard) at West Lake, which continued until 1965. Other contracts followed—a plywood plant in Quesnel, Upper Fraser Mills, Artic Mills at Bear Lake, and B.C. Forest Products at Mackenzie.

Winther broadened East Fraser's operations to include road building, hauling, and clearing of right-of-way for power lines, in addition to logging. He and his brother Eric joined Don and Jerry Flynn, Gordon Geddes, Howard Lloyd, John and Pat Martin, Gordon Swankey, and Dean Shaw in forming North Central Plywood. The mill was eventually bought by Northwood Pulp & Timber.

On September 10, 1987, Winther purchased Prince George Wood Preserving, the smallest professional sawmill in the area. Other business interests include Northern Mountain Helicopters and Baker Cable and Hooks.

Winther and his wife, Joan, have raised four children—three girls and a boy. They "get back to the land" at the W.B. Ranch near Stone Creek, where they raise Simmental cattle.

FINNING LTD.

The names Finning and Caterpillar are synonymous with the development of British Columbia. The familiar yellow equipment bearing the famous black logo has been heavily involved in the basic resource industries of the province for more than 50 years.

Incorporated on January 4, 1933, Finning evolved from two predecessor companies, the second of which was appointed Caterpillar dealer for British Columbia in 1926. Kaufman & Morrison, the original partnership formed in Vancouver in 1925, was franchised to sell the products of the C.L. Best Traction Co. throughout the province of British Columbia. A short while later the C.L. Best Company merged with its rival, Holt Manufacturing Co.

Appointed a Caterpillar dealer, the partnership was incorporated as Kaufman Morrison Ltd. Late in 1926 Kaufman withdrew from active participation, and Morrison Tractor & Equipment was formed.

Two years later Earl B. Finning entered the business. Late in 1932 Finning bought out Morrison, and Finning Tractor & Equipment Co. Ltd. was founded. Incorporated in January 1933, Finning Ltd. became a public company in 1969.

In the late 1940s increased logging and construction in the interior of the province prompted Finning to open a branch in Prince George. Opened without fanfare in 1949, it operated out of serviceman George Murray's Burden Street garage. Full branch status was achieved a year later, with the arrival of salesman Jim Mulvaney and partsman Fred Kennedy, and prompted a move to the corner of First Avenue and Victoria Street. At the time Bob Blanchette replaced Kennedy, Finning moved to 1922 First Avenue, across from the famous "planer

The Finning Ltd. facility, Prince George.

row," where it remained until 1966. Mulvaney, now retired, held the position of used equipment manager with Finning Ltd. in Vancouver.

As the forest and construction industries grew, Finning met the demand, with an expansion completed in 1951. The need for additional space in the 1960s prompted the acquisition of a seven-acre site in the PGE (now BCR) Industrial Park, south of the city, and construction began on a 50,000-square-foot, two-building complex. Incorporating ideas gained by consulting engineers in a study of other large Canadian and U.S. dealerships and patterned after Finning's 15-acre head offices and shops in Vancouver, the complex was completed at a cost of $1.25 million.

The complex was designed to service the entire central interior of the province—more than three-quarters of the total space was devoted to Caterpillar parts and repairs. Future needs were anticipated in allocating 11,000 square feet to warehouse space. In 1966, 15,000 different Caterpillar replacement parts, valued at close to one million dollars, were offered locally. Nearly 60 percent of the project cost was used to enlarge and enhance the service department, resulting in faster, more efficient repairs to Caterpillar equipment.

A further expansion, carried out in 1975, increased the complex to the present size. Attractive exterior, impressive landscaping, and highly visible signs make Finning at 1100 Pacific Street a familiar landmark on Highway 97 South. Regional manager John Desimone works with a staff of 125.

Desimone, who has been with the company for 35 years, has been part of the development of the central interior and northern half of British Columbia. An active member of the community, Desimone is involved with the Forestry Exhibition and Prince George's Oktoberfest celebration, operated by the City of Prince George and the Park and Recreation Commission.

The growth and development of the Prince George branch parallels that of the firm itself. Finning has served the basic resource industries for more than a half-century. Major markets are the forest industry, mining, engineered construction, oil and natural gas exploration and development, marine transportation, fishing, governmental agencies, and the service industries. Finning sells, leases, and services the full range of Caterpillar products and complementary equipment throughout British Columbia, Yukon Territory, the Mackenzie Valley, and the Arctic coast of the Northwest Territories.

To better serve an expanding market, Canadian and U.S. subsidiaries—Finning Allied Products in British Columbia and Alberta, and Finning Inc. in Washington—distribute Gardner-Denver air equipment and rock drills, Driltech rotary drills, Tampo compactors, and JLG high-reach equipment. Separate divisions are organized within the company to provide specialized sales and support services for Caterpillar engines and for Caterpillar lift trucks.

North American operations are headquartered in Vancouver. There are 28 full sales, parts, and service branches; 12 service depots; and 15 resident service representatives.

Finning Ltd. also sells, leases, and services Caterpillar equipment through 12 locations in the United Kingdom. Central offices in Cannock, near Birmingham, serve the industrial midlands, southwest England, and Wales. Operations in Scotland are directed from Baillieston, near Glasgow.

The firm employs more than 2,250 people throughout its territories—approximately 1,350 in the North American operations and some 900 in the United Kingdom.

Operating in the vast territory widely disparate in geographical

Left: Earl B. Finning, founder and president from 1933 to 1961.

Left center: W. Maurice Young, president from 1962 to 1980, chief executive officer from 1963 to 1984, and chairman of the board from 1963 to 1986.

Right center: D.W. Donald Lord, president and chief executive officer of Finning Ltd., Vancover, was appointed after the untimely death of Vinod K. Sood in November 1988. Lord has held many sales management and executive positions at Finning.

Right: John D. Desimone, regional manager of Finning Ltd. in Prince George.

and population characteristics, Finning has become flexible and innovative. British Columbia and the Yukon feature major mountain ranges, large river systems and many lakes, heavy forests, an abundance of minerals, and sparse population. There are long stretches of difficult terrain between small centres of population. Transportation and communication are complex and costly, affecting the company's organization and operation.

Conditions for Finning's United Kingdom operations are in sharp contrast. The territory is small in area, transportation and communication systems are well established and convenient in this

densely populated country.

Finning is recognized as a leader in the industry in its approach to new and used equipment sales. Active in equipment financing since the 1960s, the firm pioneered the concept of residual leases.

Aggressive in the trading of used equipment, Finning views used equipment as a profit opportunity rather than an occupational hazard of being in the machinery business.

Innovative in meeting the needs of its customers, not only in the introduction of new production techniques but also in adapting and modifying machines to meet particular job requirements, Finning has greatly benefited the forest industry in the Prince George area. The adaptation and modification of Caterpillar hydraulic excavators for road building, felling and bunching trees, and loading logs has added ease and efficiency to many woods operations.

Finning has become a leader in industrial training, introducing programs that are approved for certification by the province.

Finning Ltd., part of Prince George for almost 40 years, is destined to play a major role in the future of the city and area.

CANADIAN TIRE CORPORATION LIMITED

Founded in Toronto on September 15, 1922, Canadian Tire Corporation Limited is the result of John W. and Alfred J. Billes investing their combined savings of $1,800 in Hamilton Tire and Rubber Limited. Several moves and four years later, the firm became Canadian Tire Corporation.

In 1934 the first officially designated associate store opened in Hamilton, and the first catalogue was issued. By 1946 there were 116 Canadian Tire Stores. Today more than 400 stores, issuing nearly 8 million catalogues, claim a large share of the growing automotive and home market, and the Billes' small original investment is producing operating revenue in excess of $2 billion.

Tom Steadman opened the corporation's 360th store on November 19, 1982. Located on Central Street in Prince George, the 73,000-square-foot building occupies the former location of Irly Bird Building Supplies. In fact, the original structure was incorporated into the service centre

and parts storage area of the new building. The service centre waiting room, complete with children's play area, is decorated in an automotive theme, using interesting memorabilia including early hood ornaments and hubcaps.

Steadman's wife, Linda, in the dual capacity of administration and inventory control manager, is responsible for one of the largest computer systems in the city. It is used to control 25,000 different hardware, housewares, automotive, and sports products. This same computer system has been adopted by other stores in the corporation.

Canadian Tire's large inventory and merchandising techniques have had considerable impact on Prince George's business community. The firm currently employs 80 people—all but one hired in the city.

On December 5, 1983, the 10-month-old store became involved in the first strike in the history of the company. The dispute, concerning a union shop clause, re-

sulted in a stand-off between Canadian Tire (Prince George) and the Retail Clerks Union that continued until March 22, 1985. As all employees were not involved in the strike, the store continued to operate throughout the strike.

Originally from Ontario, Steadman brought his family to Prince George from Swift Current, Saskatchewan, and soon became involved in the vigorous activities of this interior British Columbian city. A member of the B.C. Festival of the Arts Committee in 1985, he was involved with the Canadian Northern Children's Festival held in Prince George during the summer of 1988, and is membership chairman of the Interior University Society.

In addition to community activities, Steadman has a keen interest in oenology and, as a collector of rare wines, keeps a very interesting cellar.

Canadian Tire Corporation Limited, founded in Toronto in 1922, opened its 360th store on Central Street in Prince George in 1982.

RUSTAD BROS. & CO. LTD.

A family-owned and -operated lumber-manufacturing company, Rustad Bros. & Co. Ltd. began as a planer mill 40 years ago. Today the computerized sawmill/planer mill complex, in the BCR Industrial Park, produces in excess of 200 million board feet of dimension lumber annually.

Carl and Mel Rustad established Rustad Bros. in July 1947 with between 15 and 20 employees in Prince George and a mill purchased in Northern California. Now 250 people work for Rustad Bros. in a state-of-the-art complex that bears very little resemblance to the original mill. President Jim Rustad (Carl's son), who has been with the firm since 1956, believes continuous change is needed to compete in today's lumber market.

In the early days it was necessary for the mill to have its own power supply to supplement that provided by the city. A diesel engine was connected directly to the planer until 1951, when a steam generator was installed to supply the steam-operated dry kiln. The planer was destroyed by fire in 1953. A second dry kiln was added when the mill was rebuilt.

In the 1960s the pulp mills came and provided an opportunity to sell chips. New machinery was required to handle barking and chipping. Following the purchase of several small sawmills, Rustad Bros. constructed a new sawmill in the BCR Industrial Park. In operation in 1967, it was followed by a new planer on the same site a year later, replacing the old River Road operation.

In spite of some setbacks—a large volume of log inventory was destroyed by fire in 1980—the company has expanded each year, using new technology to achieve higher productivity. In 1987 a new

building was constructed over the old mill and the old structure removed, providing room for a Chip'N'Saw, rebuilt with the processes in a different order.

Two new computer-operated scanning systems, the first of their kind anywhere, make it possible to get more lumber from each log—better quality wood with less wane.

Other recent changes include seven new Hyster lumber stackers, a new LeTourneau and Cat repair shop, a new Nicholson 22-inch A5 barker, and a new cut-off saw to feed the new Chip'N'Saw line, which efficiently processes wood in any diameter from 3.5 inches to 15.5 inches. Another line is capable of processing large logs, some measuring up to 58 inches in diameter.

Future plans include a new

Since 1967 Rustad Bros. has been located at the BCR Indusrial Park.

trimmer optimizer and a new grade reader.

Rustad Bros. has shown leadership in the industry, offering innovative changes and active participation in lumber-related organizations. Mel and Jim Rustad have served terms as president of the Northern Interior Lumber Association, and Jim is currently chairman of the Council of Forest Industries of British Columbia.

In addition to domestic sales of dimension products, Rustad Bros. & Co. Ltd. supplies an international market, including the United States, Japan, Australia, and the United Kingdom. "You name the place, we've probably shipped there," says president Jim Rustad.

EXCEL TRANSPORTATION INC.

Moving wood chips to the mill is the first important step in pulp and paper manufacture. Transportation methods vary from one part of Canada to another, and are determined by the particular terrain, physical features, climate, and distance involved.

While the railway was the main method of transportation for wood chips in the 1960s, the competitiveness in the trucking industry for chip hauling became more apparent in the 1970s and 1980s. The chip-trucking industry has increased dramatically over the past decade to where it is now a major transportation factor in the wood

communities. Of the firm's 100 employees, 70 live and work in Prince George and 30 work out of the Terrace terminal. Chips are hauled from the Prince George and Terrace areas to distances exceeding 100 miles.

In the Prince George area, chip trucks bearing the Excel Transportation logo are familiar sights. The sheer size of these vehicles makes meeting one on a road for the first time a memorable experience.

The company name became Excel Transportation Inc. in 1985, reflecting the corporate image of service excellence. Edworthy, a longtime resident familiar with

make this high capacity possible.

In addition to chips, Excel Transportation hauls hog fuel (bark, sawdust, and shavings) to the pulp mills, utilizing self-unloading trailers and B trains.

Projected demands for pulp, paper, and paperboard by the world market will mean growth in employment and increased activity in transportation.

Edworthy's future plans include further growth of Excel Transportation and diversification to other areas of the industry.

In discussing the rapid growth and success of his company, Edworthy is quick to recognize the con-

The first B Train trailer, used for hauling chips, has been employed extensively by Excel Transportation.

Pictured here is the latest trailer design, conceived and manufactured by Les Edworthy. These trailers now comprise the majority of Excel's fleet.

chip and hog fuel industry in the northern interior of British Columbia.

Edworthy Enterprises Ltd. was formed in 1973 by Les Edworthy, who recognized the potential for trucks that could haul wood chips to the pulp mills. The company has grown with the industry— from one truck to a fleet of 45.

Thirty-three of these trucks operate in the Prince George area and 12 are based at Terrace, generating a payroll of $3.7 million in the two

both the transportation and the pulp and paper industries, realized that sawmills wanted the most cost-effective service possible and pioneered the development of a specialized trailer, building the prototype in the firm's fabricating shop.

His early experience in the pulp mill industry as a welder and fabricator served him well during the design and modification stages of the project. While the first unit had a capacity of 104,000 pounds gross vehicle weight, several modifications have resulted in the model currently in use, which has a gross vehicle capacity of 140,000 pounds. Two separate trailers

tributions made by his employees, most of whom are local residents, stressing that people are Excel's most important asset. Several drivers have been with the company since its inception.

A family man with three children, Edworthy takes pride in Prince George, lending personal and corporate support to many community projects. Of course his pride extends to Excel Transportation Inc.—a Prince George success story.

HUSKY OIL

The Husky Oil refinery in Prince George was designed and built to fill a market void that existed in central British Columbia in the mid-1960s. With the nearest refinery 300 miles away in Taylor, British Columbia, and two major pulp mills in the Prince George area creating an immediate market for fuel oil, a local refinery was the obvious answer.

From the beginning the refinery, which was built and originally owned by Union Oil Company of Canada Ltd., had to satisfy a series of rigid demands. First, the refinery had to operate in winter temperatures as low as 40 degrees below zero. Second, the plant had to produce gasoline and diesel fuels suitable for an 80-degree climatic variation between summer and winter. Third, because it was situated near the confluence of two important salmon rivers, the Nechako and Fraser, the refinery needed a highly efficient treating system to ensure that waste products were safely contained. And fourth, because its capacity of only 7,500 barrels per day was relatively small, capital outlay and operating costs had to be kept exceptionally low if the refinery was to be profitable.

Foundations were ready for major equipment in the early spring of 1967. The refinery went on stream in September 1967, a few days ahead of schedule, and was operating at rated capacity within two weeks.

Since 1967 the Husky Oil refinery has been serving Prince George's petroleum needs with high-quality products at a reasonable price.

The economics did not work out quite as planned. A contract was signed with the pulp mills to supply heavy fuel oil at a rate competitive to natural gas, which was expected to rise in price. The price of natural gas never did increase—if anything, it kept going down—which made the profits of the refinery marginal for a period of time.

Husky Oil bought the refining and marketing assets of Union Oil on November 1, 1976, and immediately set out to make the refinery more profitable. A catalytic cracking unit installation and crude unit expansion were completed in November 1978, which boosted crude capacity to 10,000 barrels per day and improved the product mix by increasing the yield of gasoline and diesel fuel.

An immediate result of this program was more jobs. The maintenance crew tripled, and more people were added to the tank farm and process department. Today the refinery provides direct employment for more than 80 people and has a significant effect on the economy of the Prince George region. For residents and businesses in Prince George, the refinery provides high-quality, reasonably priced products that meet all the requirements of current technology.

Community involvement has always been a priority for the refinery employees. John Wesch, refinery manager from the start-up in 1967 until 1974, served on the hospital board and was a member of the Prince George Rotary Club. Geoff Bonser, refinery manager from 1980 to 1988, is the 1987-1988 president of the Prince George/Nechako Rotary Club and was a director of the Prince George Symphony Orchestra from 1980 through 1985.

The Prince George refinery has continually been upgraded and improved and is an efficiently run refinery for its size, making it an important part of Husky Oil's overall downstream operations.

Husky Oil was started in Cody, Wyoming, 50 years ago and is now an integrated Canadian oil and gas company engaged in exploration, development, production, marketing, and transportation of crude oil and natural gas in addition to the refining of crude oil and the wholesale and retail marketing of refined petroleum products. Upstream operations are located in Western Canada, off the east coast of Canada, and in the Beaufort Sea. International interests are located in Indonesia and Senegal. Downstream operations extend from Western Canada through to the Ontario/Quebec border.

Husky is a privately held company controlled by two principal shareholders, NOVA Corporation of Alberta and Hong Kong-based Hutchison Whampoa Limited, both of which are publicly listed and traded.

SCHULTZ PONTIAC BUICK LTD.

From a temporary location in a service station at Fifth Avenue and Carney Street, Schultz Pontiac Buick Ltd. has, in fewer than 20 years, grown to become the largest General Motors automotive dealership outside of Vancouver.

E.R. "Ernie" Schultz founded the dealership on April 15, 1969, with his son Jack as the first employee. A member of a large family, the elder Schultz was raised on a farm near Bashaw, Alberta, a farming community just south of Edmonton, where he moved as a young man. It was there he married Audrey Lees, born in Bramshot, England. The couple had three children, two girls and a boy. Schultz' career with General Motors began at Edmonton Motors, continued at Hood Motors and at Don Wheaton Chevrolet, where he became manager. Jack, studying for his degree in business administration at Northern Alberta Institute of Technology in Edmonton, worked part time for his father.

Learning that Prince George was without a Buick-Pontiac dealership, Schultz obtained the franchise and moved west. Exhibiting uncanny foresight, his first plan was to establish an auto mall. Discovering the city was not quite ready for this concept, he proceeded to acquire and re-zone land at 1111 Central Street and construction began. (It is interesting to note that auto malls are now gaining in popularity, with the Richmond Auto Mall as a good example of this merchandising method.)

After operating sales from the Fifth and Carney location, the service department from Kingston Street, and body shop from Quinn Street location, the new building opened in March 1970. The body shop remained on Quinn Street

E.R. Schultz brought Prince George its first Pontiac Buick dealership in 1969.

for five years before it was moved to its present location, 1975 First Avenue.

Quickly gaining acceptance, the new dealership grew, and as demand increased the inventory, space became a problem. Rather than scatter the operation, the challenge was met by building up. The tiered parkade, built in 1976, provided a unique solution to the problem and offered the added bonus of protecting vehicles from the elements.

In 1984 Ernie Schultz retired and his son became president. Jack and his wife, the former Susan Phillips from Edmonton, by this time had two children, a son and a daughter. Presently the family is very involved in the business and the community. Jack has served as president of the local auto dealers' association and on the board of General Motors' Western Regional Dealers' Council. Susan, a University of Alberta home economics graduate, is a well-known

Jack Schultz assumed the presidency of Schultz Pontiac Buick when his father, founder E.R. Schultz, retired in 1984.

fashion consultant.

Over the years the staff has grown from 40 to almost 80, creating an annual payroll of $2 million. The success of Schultz Pontiac Buick can be attributed to innovative management and marketing. A good example of local ingenuity in marketing is the P.G. Hauler—a pickup truck with a difference. The people at Schultz took a GMC S-15 four-cylinder, five-speed half-ton and, by adding mag wheels, cloth upholstery, and distinctive sports striping, gave it a new identity and created a market for it. More than 100 were sold in 1987, with orders coming from as far away as Vancouver.

Hart Highway Motors was acquired in 1986, offering a GM service centre and body shop to the residents of that area. This is also the site for Jack Schultz Suzuki, selling Suzuki trucks and Forsa cars.

Schultz Pontiac Buick Ltd. is a vital part of Prince George's economy.

CARIBOO CENTRAL INTERIOR RADIO INC.
CENTRAL INTERIOR CABLEVISION LTD.

"This is CFBV, Smithers!" With those words in 1963, founder and president Ron East introduced community-based radio broadcasting to this Bulkey Valley community and launched the first phase of the far-reaching Cariboo Central Radio Network.

For a time CFBV operated out of a modest bungalow in downtown Smithers. Now located in a modern broadcast facility, CFBV still maintains the original informal style so appreciated by listeners.

CFBV is unique in a technical sense—completely automated from the beginning. Responsible for technological planning and innovations is partner Stan Davis of S.W. Davis Broadcast Technical Services Limited of Vancouver. East and Davis have been a highly successful team for 25 years.

It soon became evident that there was a need for a similar service to Burns Lake (120 kilometres east). In order to provide a clear signal in the mountainous terrain, a satellite transmitter was established, creating the first link in the future network.

The rapid growth experienced by Prince George in the mid-1960s prompted East, Davis, and a group of investors, including George Baldwin, Q.C., serving as secretary, to seek a new radio licence. CJCI commenced broadcasting in August 1970 from the penthouse of The Inn of the North with a staff of 12. Today a staff of 32 maintains 24-hour service from CI's broadcast centre on Third Avenue.

It is the only radio station in Western Canada to employ total computerization. This degree of technology used in presentation and dissemination of news via a telex network won CJCI the Canadian Association of Broadcasters' Award for Innovation in Broadcasting in 1972.

CIVH in Vanderhoof went on the air in 1973, and two years later the Smithers-Burns Lake and Prince George-Vanderhoof companies combined to apply for repeater transmitters to serve Fort St. James, Fraser Lake, Granisle, Houston, and Hazelton, creating a nine-transmitter radio service serving the majority of the population along the 300 miles of Highway 16 West.

CIBC-FM, added to the company as a jointly held licence with CJCI, commenced broadcasting on October 25, 1983, and also operates a repeater transmitter service to the Vanderhoof/Nechako Valley area.

The Cariboo Central Interior Radio Network provides an invaluable service to Prince George and the Nechako and Bulkey Valley communities.

President East joined with manager Herb Maxwell, secretary George Baldwin, Q.C., and first board members John Boates (Quesnel), Bob Leckie (Williams Lake), and Stan Davis (Vancouver) to form Central Interior CableVision Ltd. in 1973. It is a public company with shares widely held by residents of the region. CableVision ser-

Above, left to right: R.A. East, S.W. Davis, G.W. Baldwin, Q.C.

vice to Prince George commenced in December 1975 and now includes systems in Quesnel, Williams Lake, and 100 Mile House. General manager Carole McNally, technical plant manager Bert Verheyde, and office manager Sharon Butler operate the network from the CableVision Centre in Prince George. The firm offers 21 television channels, including all popular Canadian and American networks, an all-movie channel, an all-sports channel, plus the Nashville and Arts & Entertainment networks, and Cable 10, the community-access channel co-ordinated by Bill Opdahl.

East is past president of the B.C. Association of Broadcasters, director of the Canadian Cable TV Research Institute and the Canadian Bureau of Broadcast Measurement and Canadian Broadcast News, and in 1976 was named Broadcaster of the Year by the British Columbia Association of Broadcasters.

George Baldwin, a well-known Prince George lawyer, died in an automobile accident on September 30, 1977.

CANFOR PRINCE GEORGE PULP AND PAPER MILLS

The occasion of Canfor's 50th anniversary invites the telling of the company's history, with special emphasis on the 22 years of the Prince George operations.

It is a story of people and trees brought together by two entrepreneurs who created a small enterprise that has emerged as one of Canada's major forest products companies.

Canfor's manufacturing operations extend from Vancouver Island to northern Alberta. Prince George Pulp and Paper, opened in 1966, was the first pulp mill to be located in the great forest reserve of north-central British Columbia. A sister mill, Intercontinental Pulp, began operations two years later.

In the late 1930s John G. Prentice and L.L.G. "Poldi" Bentley, friends and brothers-in-law, were involved in a family textile firm operating in their native Austria and in Czechoslovakia. In March 1938 the threat of war prompted them to bring their families to British Columbia, leaving behind personal property and the textile company. In a very short time they had used the small amount of capital they had managed to bring to open Pacific Veneer in New Westminster.

In 1939 the war they had feared became a reality, and it was creating a need for wood products. Britain, unable to obtain European wood supplies, looked to North America. Pacific Veneer became a supplier of plywood for aviation and marine production. Later it produced construction plywood for the rebuilding of war-torn Europe.

In 1940 the company bought the failing Eburne Saw Mills Limited on the Fraser River in Vancouver. A few years later, to secure a supply of raw material, three small Fraser Valley logging operations were purchased, forming

the base of today's Mainland Logging Division.

The acquisition of timber rights in the Nimpkish Valley on Vancouver Island in 1944 led to the formation of the Englewood Logging Division. Included in the purchase was a small firm called Canadian Forest Products Ltd. In 1947 all operations were organized under that name.

The Eburne purchase made the company a shareholder in Seaboard Lumber Sales Ltd., giving it improved access to offshore markets. Next came a Canada-wide building materials distribution network, using the name "Canfor," which today stretches from Nanaimo to St. John's, Newfoundland.

Seeking new opportunities, the firm then acquired a pulp mill at Port Mellon on Howe Sound in 1951, followed by a number of acquisitions in and around Grande Prairie, Alberta, in 1955 and Chetwynd, British Columbia, in 1963.

As Prentice and Bentley worked to acquire the timber base so necessary for growth, they were also attracting a skilled and ded-

Aerial photo of Canfor's mills today, with the city in the background, Intercontinental Pulp at centre, Prince George Pulp at left, and the mills' effluent treatment facility in the foreground.

icated work force led by an outstanding management team.

Bill McMahan, a veteran British Columbia lumberman, joined the company in 1940 and became manager of logging operations and later vice-president and a director. He in turn hired Russell Mills, who took over the Englewood Logging Division.

In the early 1960s two senior executives, John Liersch, who had joined the firm in 1961 and was to become vice-president, and Tom Wright, chief forester, helped convince the provincial government of the need to construct a pulp mill in Prince George to utilize the wood then being wasted by the local sawmills or left behind in the forests after logging. They demonstrated that only 25 percent of the timber in a stand was leaving for market; the remaining 75 percent was wasted.

B.C. Lands and Forests Minister Ray Williston came up with a plan to utilize this leftover wood. The new system of pulpwood harvesting licences forced dramatic changes on interior logging as a pulp-mill economy was superimposed on the existing sawmill economy.

In 1962 the company was granted Pulp Harvesting Area No. 1, an 8-million-acre tract of land in the Prince George area. With the PHA came certain conditions that necessitated finding a partner to assure a market.

A joint venture with Reed Paper Group Limited of the United Kingdom, the $84-million, 750-ton-per-day Prince George Pulp and Paper Limited mill was officially opened by Premier W.A.C. Bennett on August 27, 1966. Speakers at the opening included Prince George Mayor Garvin Dezell; W.E. Soles, president of both Prince George Pulp and Paper Limited and Anglo-Canadian Pulp & Paper Mills Limited; L.L.G. Bentley, chairman of Prince George Pulp and Paper Limited and vice-president of Canadian Forest Products; Cecil King, chairman of Reed Paper Group Limited; and Ray Williston, Minister of Lands, Forests, and Water Resources for British Columbia. Vice-president and general manager John Gutherie and staff hosted 400 guests, many flown to

Canfor's Prince George Pulp and Paper Mills won St. John Ambulance's Award for Best Program during Occupational Health and Safety Week in 1987. St. John Ambulance representative Bob McDermit presents the award to general manager John Dougherty, surrounded by members of joint safety committees.

Left: Premier W.A.C. Bennett officially opened Prince George Pulp and Paper on August 27, 1966.

Right: Wood chips are the raw material from which kraft pulp is made. Here a truck unloads the fast way at Intercontinental Pulp, a Canfor company.

Prince George on a special charter flight from Vancouver.

At the time Prince George Pulp and Paper had the largest initial capacity of any mill ever built in Canada, and was the largest employer in the area, surpassing 500 employees and an annual payroll in excess of $4 million.

Producing a wide range of bleached market pulps and a very high grade of kraft paper for use in the manufacture of multiwall bags, Prince George Pulp and Paper has made a lasting impact, economically and socially, on the community.

A second pulp mill, Intercontinental, a joint venture with Reed and Feldmuehle of Germany, built on the same site as Prince George Pulp and Paper at a cost of $60 million, went into production in May 1968. The joint-venture partners also acquired several small sawmilling and logging companies in the Prince George area that were then consolidated at Isle Pierre and Fort St. James. Today all these operations are wholly owned by

Canfor.

Located at the confluence of the Fraser and Nechako rivers, the two mills are highly automated and computerized, using the Nechako River as a source of pure, fresh water essential to production of clean pulp.

The Prince George Pulp and Paper mill has an annual production capacity of 170,000 tons of prime market softwood pulp, plus 100,000 tons of high-quality kraft paper. Intercontinental Pulp has an annual production capacity of 230,000 tons of prime market softwood pulp. Both mills operate under the direction of John Dougherty.

The skill and dedication of Prince George Pulp and Paper mills employees ensure that the operations run at peak efficiency, enabling Canfor to produce consistently high-quality products and maintain its reputation for reliable service.

As Canfor celebrates its 50th anniversary, it can be justifiably proud of the Prince George mill operations—Prince George Pulp and Paper Ltd. and Intercontinental Pulp.

NORTHERN STEEL LTD.

Back of the beating hammer
By which the steel is wrought,
Back of the workshop's clamor
The seeker may find the thought.
from The Thinker
by Berton Braley

Performing many functions, steel has played and still has an important role in northern development. Northern Steel Ltd. and Kodiak Steel Industries Ltd. serve the forestry, mining, and construction industries in this area.

Doug Coppin and Fritz Hausot founded Northern Steel Ltd. in 1977. Coppin's extensive experience with a national steel company and Hausot's background in steel fabricating resulted in a firm tailored to service logging and sawmill equipment with an awareness

of local needs.

Located in a 5,000-square-foot building on Milwaukee Way in the BCR Industrial Park, the firm began with three employees. Many early projects were seasonal, the staff fluctuating between 30 and 120.

The burgeoning business soon required construction of the present 25,000-square-foot facility at 9565 Rock Island Road. Then the most modern fabricating shop in British Columbia, it was the most certified in the northern part of the province.

Larger premises sparked diversification; soon Northern Steel was involved in general fabricating and service to the forestry, mining, pulp, chemical, and construction industries. Facilities were upgraded to

complete machine shop services.

The largest Prince George fabricating supplier for the Northeast Coal Development at Tumbler Ridge, Northern Steel built access bridges to both the Quintette and Bullmoose coal mines.

Exhibiting the business acumen that sets northern entrepreneurs apart, Coppin and Hausot promoted their firm in Vancouver and other large centres, securing markets in British Columbia, Alberta, and the United States. One project involves building components for a U.S. chemical plant.

For the company's future, Coppin sees continued growth and expansion to accommodate new equipment. A Prince George success story, Northern Steel Ltd. is a local company that grew!

KODIAK STEEL INDUSTRIES LTD.

Doug Coppin and Fritz Hausot had long been aware of the need for a local company to serve northern industrial clients, a company aware of local conditions. The closing of a Vancouver-based steel supply firm provided them with the opportunity they needed.

Coppin sought out longtime friend Bob MacPhee, a man with nearly 30 years' experience in the steel-distribution field. Facilities on Pacific Street in the BCR Industrial Park were leased, inventories brought in, and Kodiak Steel Industries Ltd. became a reality on February 15, 1984.

A considerably reduced market caused by a province-wide economic downturn made Kodiak's first year a difficult one. It was a year fraught with problems, but each was ultimately resolved.

The end of 1984 saw Kodiak Steel Industries firmly established. It was recognized as the most reli-

able steel source in northern British Columbia. The acceptance and support of the many local businesses has been the company's success.

The years 1985 and 1986 were marked by consolidation and growth. Additional processing equipment resulted in improved customer service. Inventories were enlarged and diversified. The percentage of materials supplied in a pre-processed state grew steadily, and the superb quality of Kodiak's work became firmly established. The "family" of four grew to 10, with the largest increase in the warehouse staff.

To better handle its inventory, credit, sales, and purchasing, Kodiak embraced computer technology in 1986. The arrival of the in-house computer meant changes, but soon everyone was involved and could not imagine returning to manual methods.

The year 1987 saw continued growth, and everything was proceeding on a steady course when Kodiak's leased facilities were purchased by a competitor, making it necessary to find a new home—and quickly. The move to larger premises at 9714 Milwaukee Way in the BCR Industrial Park was carried out in August 1987. It was immediately apparent that the new facilities increased Kodiak's service to its wide range of customers.

A proud member of the community, Copping looks forward to contributing to the growth and prosperity of Prince George and northern areas.

INTERIOR WAREHOUSING LTD.

Incorporated in 1958, Interior Warehousing Ltd. came into being when Jim Perry and partners purchased 97 Transfer from Gordon Sales. Trucks bearing the 97 Transfer name continued to be familiar sights on the roads and highways around Prince George as the company, under Perry's direction, expanded and prospered.

When Perry made the decision to establish Interior Warehousing Ltd., he sold 97 Transfer to his employees. The locally owned and operated independent warehousing firm opened for business in 1969.

The first warehousing and distribution centre, located at 1989 First Avenue, almost immediately proved to be too small for the fast-growing company, and a site was secured at 1024 Great Street in the BCR Industrial Park. Following completion of the 31,000-square-foot building, the move was made in 1971.

As agents for Cottrell Transport, Inc., Interior Warehousing began servicing an ever-increasing number of clients in the central interior, offering receiving, storage, inventory, and delivery for everything from chemicals and paper to food products. Today 11 transport units, bearing both Interior Warehousing Ltd. and Cottrell names, maintain a very busy schedule throughout the area.

A second warehouse on River Road, on a CN spur line, offering 20,000 square feet of distribution and storage, is the main distribution centre. Built with the capacity to accommodate eight boxcars, this warehouse offers indoor handling of products—a prime consideration when the temperature dips below zero. In fact, it is the most modern storage and handling operation in northern British Columbia.

While Perry makes the business of warehousing appear effortless, it is an extremely involved operation requiring extreme care and efficiency. Of course, knowing almost everyone in the area helps, too.

Interior Warehousing is a family business. Perry's sons, Chris and Mike, are now involved in the company. The delivery of chemicals is one of their areas of responsibility. The tightly run operation

Right: As an agent for Cottrell Transport, Inc., Interior Warehousing Ltd. operates a delivery fleet of 11 vehicles.

Below: Interior Warehousing Ltd., whose warehousing and distribution centre is located in the BCR and CNR Industrial Park, offers receiving, storage, inventory, and delivery for everything from chemicals and paper to food products.

has a staff of 12, most of whom are longtime employees. Job sharing has been introduced, with Gerda Kordlek and Lois Englesjord, both with 15 years of service, handling office responsibilities.

The senior Perry, a well-respected member of the business community, is very involved in other aspects of Prince George growth. He is past president of the Central Interior Transportation Club and the Central Interior Loggers Association, the latter founded by him in 1964. He and his wife, Anne, are active members of the Loyal Order of Elks and Royal Purple. Their country home, enhanced by Anne's well-known love for decorating and gardening, is often the scene of social gatherings. Together they enjoy cross-country skiing, tennis, and a little golf.

When the subject of retiring is broached, Jim Perry smiles and shakes his head, saying, "Not for a while yet."

The Grand Trunk Pacific Railway bridge makes way for this sternwheeler in 1914. Courtesy, Provincial Archives of British Columbia

PATRONS

The following individuals, companies, and organizations have made a valuable commitment to the quality of this publication. Windsor Publications and the Prince George Chamber of Commerce gratefully acknowledge their participation in *Prince George: Rivers, Railways, and Timber.*

B.C. Chemicals Ltd.
B.C. Forest Service
    Prince George Forest Region
B.C. Lands
B.C. Telephone Company
Canadian Tire Corporation Limited
Canfor Prince George Pulp and
    Paper Mills
Cariboo Central Interior Radio Inc.
    Central Interior Cablevision Ltd.
The College of New Caledonia

Crossroads Construction
Deloitte Haskins & Sells
Deron Forest Technik Ltd.
Domtar Chemicals Group
    Wood Preserving Division
East Fraser Logging Ltd.
Excel Transportation Inc.
Finning Ltd.
Holiday Inn-Prince George
Howat Insurance Brokers Inc.
Husky Oil
Inland Natural Gas Co. Ltd.
Interior Warehousing Ltd.
Kodiak Steel Industries Ltd.
Lakeland Mills Ltd.
Linden Fabricating & Engineering
    P.G. Ltd.
Northern Steel Ltd.
Northland Plymouth Chrysler Ltd.
Northwood Pulp and Timber
    Limited

Novak Bros. Ltd.
    Dunkley Lumber Ltd.
Overwaitea Foods
The Pas Lumber Company
The Prince George Citizen
The Prince George Regional
    Hospital
Prince George Warehousing Co. Ltd.
    Northern Interior Fastfrate Ltd.
Prince George Wood Preserving
    Ltd.
Reed Stenhouse Ltd.
Rustad Bros. & Co. Ltd.
Schultz Pontiac Buick Ltd.
Touche Ross & Co.

Partners in Progress of *Prince George: Rivers, Railways, and Timber.* The histories of these companies and organizations appear in Chapter VIII, beginning on page 119.

Above: Piles of lumber were used for seating at this ballgame on the Fort George townsite in 1912. Courtesy, Provincial Archives of British Columbia

Right: Sports day at King George V elementary school is observed by proud parents in 1920. Courtesy, Fraser-Fort George Regional Museum

In 1939, this natural ice arena was constructed on the south east corner of Sixth Avenue and Quebec Street at a total cost of $15,000. In 1956 it collapsed suddenly under a heavy load of snow. Courtesy, Fraser-Fort George Regional Museum

Harold Moffat, right, presents the Kelly Cup to Bill Kirschke in 1956. Courtesy, Fraser-Fort George Regional Museum

BIBLIOGRAPHY

BOOKS AND ESSAYS

Akrigg, G.P.V. and Helen B. *British Columbia Chronicle 1778-1846, Adventures by Land and Sea.* Discovery Press, 1975.

——————. *British Columbia Chronicle 1847-1871, Gold and Colonists.* Discovery Press, 1977.

Anderson, Alexander Caufield (J.P.). *Notes on North-Western America.* Montreal: Mitchell and Wilson, Printers, 1876.

B.C. 60 Years of Progress. Volume 2.

Bancroft, The Works of Hubert Howe. Volume xxxii, 1792-1887. San Francisco: The History Company, Publishers, 1887.

Begg, Alex. *History of British Columbia from its Earliest Discovery to the Present Time.* Toronto: 1894.

——————. *History of the North-West.* Volume 1. Toronto: 1894.

Bumby, Anna. "The Sales Campaign of George J. Hammond and the Natural Resources Security Company." College of New Caledonia, local history seminar research essay. Spring 1981.

Caine, Martin and Errol. Pioneer interview. Tape recording, Prince George Public Library.

Canadian Encyclopedia. Hurtig Publishers Ltd., 1985.

Carter, Susan. Pioneer interview. Tape recording, Prince George Public Library.

Clark, Alice. Pioneer interview. Tape recording, Prince George Public Library.

Cline, Gloria Griffen. *Peter Skene Ogden and the Hudson's Bay Company.* University of Oklahoma Press, 1974.

Coccola, Nicolas. *The Life and Work of Rev. Father Nicolas Coccola, OMI.* As related to Denys Nelson, 1924.

College of New Caledonia. Various documents of the Department of Indian Affairs.

Dennison, Robert C. "The Role of Education in Prince George, 1910-1960." Local history seminar research project, 1981.

Devereau, F.A. *Survey of Reserve No. 1 situated on the right bank of the Fraser River adjoining the northern boundary of the Hudson Bay Co. claim at Fort George.* CNC Library.

Downs, Art. *Paddlewheels on the Frontier.* Gray's Publishing Ltd., 1972.

Edwards, Margaret H. *A Bibliography of B.C.* 1975.

Friesen, J. and Ralston, H.K. *Historical Essays on B.C.* Toronto: McClelland and Stewart Ltd., 1976.

Gosnell, Edward. *A Great Britain on the Pacific.* Toronto: McClelland and Stewart Ltd., 1976.

Henness, Diamond. "Indians of Canada." National Museum of Canada, Anthropological Series No. 15, Fifth edition, 1960.

Holmes, Neil Bradford. "The Promotion of Early Growth in a Western Canadian City: A Case Study of Prince George, B.C., 1909-1915." University of British Columbia, essay submitted in partial fulfillment of the requirements for the degree of Bachelor of Arts, 1974.

Howay, Frederick William. *British Columbia: The Making of a Province.* Ryerson Press, 1928.

Kennedy, Jane. Pioneer interview. Tape recording, Prince George Public Library.

Lay, Douglas. *Fraser River Tertiary Drainage-history in relation to Placer-gold Deposits.* B.C. Department of Mines, 1940.

Leonard, Frank. "Grand Trunk Pacific and the Establishment of the City of Prince George, 1911-1915." B.C. Studies, Autumn 1984.

McKelvie, Bruce Alistair. *Tales of Conflict: Indian-White Murders and Massacres in Pioneer B.C.* Heritage House Publishing Co. Ltd., 1985.

McMicking, Thomas. *Overland from Canada to British Columbia.* The University of B.C., 1981.

McNaughton, Margaret. *Overland to Cariboo: An Eventful Journey of Canadian Pioneers to the Gold Fields of B.C. in 1862.* Toronto: William Briggs, 1896.

Malzahn, Manfred R. "Merchants and the Evolution of the North Cariboo of British Columbia, 1908-1933." McGill University, Department of Geography, 1979.

Miller, Dawn. "Short of the Mark." Local history seminar, research on education services, 1981.

Moles, Garvin. *Local History in Prince George: A Research Guide.* Local History Committee of the Prince George Public Library.

Morice, Father Adrien Gabriel. *The History of the Northern Interior of British Columbia.* Interior Stationery Ltd., Smithers, 1978.

Ormsby, Margaret. *British Columbia: a History.* MacMillan of Canada, 1971.

Oswald, Cathie. "Stumpage, Royalty and a Pulp Mill Proposal, Prince George, 1920." Local history seminar essay, 1981.

Palmer, H. Spencer. *B.C. Williams Lake and Cariboo Topographical Reports on the Portions of the Williams Lake and Cariboo Districts and on the Fraser River From Fort Alexander to Fort George.* New Westminster: Royal Engineers Press, 1863.

Pond, Peter. *Five Fur Traders of the Northwest.* The diaries of John Macdonell, Archibald N. McLeod, Hugh Fairies and Thomas Conner. University of Minnesota Press, 1933.

Runnalls, Rev. Francis Edwin. *A History of Prince George.* Fraser Fort George Museum Society, 1985.

Sage, Walter Noble. *Sir James Douglas and British Columbia.* The University of Toronto Press, 1930.

——————. "Life at a Fur Trading Post in B.C. a Century Ago." *The Washington Historical Quarterly,* Volume xxv, No. 1, January 1934.

——————. "New Caledonia the Siberia of the Fur Trade." *The Beaver,* Summer 1956: 24.

Simpson's Journal 1824-1825, Fur Trade and Empire. Edited by Frederick Merk. Harvard University Press, 1931.

Steventon, Bob. "The Origins and Background of the Wenner-Gren B.C. Development Project." Local history seminar essay, 1981.

A Summary Report of Development Possibilities in the Central Region of British Columbia. Government of B.C., Department of Economic Development, 1976.

Talbot, R.A. *The making of a Great Canadian Railway.*

Wade, Mark S. *The Overlanders of '62.*

Washburn, Stanley. *Trails, Trappers and Tenderfeet in the New Empire of Western Canada.* London: Andrew Melrose, 1912.

West, Willis J. "The BX and the Rush to Fort George." *British Columbia Historical Quarterly,* Volume xiii, July/August 1949.

Williams, Ted. Pioneer interview. Tape recording, Prince George Public Library.

Wilson, Peter. Pioneer interview. Tape recording, Prince George Public Library.

Woodward, F.M. Thesis on B.C. History and related subjects. 1971.

NEWSPAPERS

The Citizen
Fort George Herald
Prince George Daily News
Prince George Leader
Prince George Post
Prince George Progress
Prince George Star
Vancouver Province

INDEX

GENERAL INDEX
Boldfaced entries indicate sidebars.
Italicized numbers indicate illustrations.

Photo by Bob Clarke